# Earn Money While Losing Weight With Jesus

## How to Advertise Your Products, Services, & Content Like the Big Players

EDWARD J. BALDEGA

# TABLE OF CONTENTS

# INTRODUCTION

Gotcha! Did the title, "Earn Money While Losing Weight With Jesus," catch your eye? The answer is probably a BIG YES. The catchy title is just one method to grab an audience's attention, but there are many more. We will talk about them in this book.

The title is what first interested you in this book, which is the first step. But let me tell you what I have learned about businesses, and how they hook a consumer apart from the store name, for example. There is an art to convincing you, the consumer, to buy a product, and I will talk about many of them in this book.

The first thing to think about is why you buy something. Is it because you like shiny things and want to collect them? That is a valid reason since many of us collect items from figurines to stamps. However, there is another reason, which is necessity. For example, we all need clothes; however, we choose our clothing styles based on varying factors such as age, image, and purpose. Businesses consider all of those reasons when advertising their product(s).

## MARKETING TACTICS

Companies use various techniques—Marketing Techniques—to sell their product, and there are many of these, because not everyone is looking for the same thing. Likewise, not everyone goes searching for a product for the same reason. Therefore, a business needs to understand its target audience. For example, a 20-year-old woman will look for a completely different clothing style than a 50-year-old woman. Or, both may be searching for the same type of clothing but for different reasons. For example, the younger person may want lounge pants, to look casual while out and about, while an older person may want the same pants for literally lounging around the house. Since it would be nearly impossible for the business owner to speak to everyone worldwide, the company would have to implement various techniques to determine what their target audience wants and why. Then they'd have to work to provide both of those things.

Often, someone will start a business based on the entrepreneur's desire to provide a product to a specific group of people. They might believe that there are enough members of a group of people, and that those who do purchase the product will convince others to buy the same product even if they are not of the same mindset. The best example is religion-based companies, which determine that enough people share the same belief system to keep the company profitable. However, these companies can employ various marketing tactics for their target market-based business to attract consumers outside their target audience.

This book's twelve chapters will be broken down into the following: Chapters 1 - 4 will be about money-making companies; Chapters 5 - 8 about weight-loss companies; and Chapters 9 - 12 about companies selling religion. Keep in mind while reading that most, if not all, companies use multiple marketing tactics. When it comes to specialty companies with a narrower target audience, it is especially vital to utilize every marketing tactic available. Profit is essential to running a business; the profit shrinks if the target audience is too small. Therefore, finding ways to add to consumer interest is of utmost importance.

# Chapter 1

---

# INVESTMENT FIRMS

The world of finance, especially investment firms, is a competitive market. Investment firms manage, sell, and market funds to the public. They earn profits from buying and selling shares, property, cash, and other resources for their clients (Chen, 2020). So if you want to dabble in the stock market for money, or to set up a retirement fund, finding the right investment firm is the first step. Because of the competitiveness within investment firms, the marketing tactics of the ones with higher ratings are top-notch. These companies understand their clients, and know how to build their client base. You can learn a lot from these companies' marketing strategies, especially the tried and true methods of successfully advertising a company.

## ROBINHOOD

Robinhood is a relatively new investment firm in the world of finance. The company was founded in April 2015. The founders recognized that the investment market benefits the wealthy, and the financial market is generally an incomprehensible, misunderstood entity to most of the population. So the founders of Robinhood decided to democratize finance, giving everyone access to the financial markets. In addition, Robinhood made investments friendly, approachable, and understandable. As a result, the company is a safe place to create an understanding of financial tools for both experts and newcomers.

Robinhood founders seem to use the 4A Model of Marketing from The Marketing Mix to gain new customers while keeping the existing ones happy. Using this approach, the founders of Robinhood looked at the world of finance through the eyes of potential customers to know what would work. This marketing approach is the same that Coca-Cola has used for years. The components that stand out from this marketing tool in Robinhood's strategies are affordability, accessibility (through affordability), and awareness.

## Accessibility and Affordability

Robinhood's business strategy has made the financial market affordable to more than just the wealthy. Through its affordability, it has become accessible to more of the population. There is another level of the accessibility component, which is customer convenience. By utilizing an app and making their services available through a completely online system, they have made it more convenient for customers to use their services and access the financial market. As a result, trading and selling on the stock market have never been easier.

Everyone knows about the financial market and the endless possibilities to earn money. However, for years it has been the golden ring of finance on this merry-go-round called life; few understand the process, making it intimidating and left to the wealthy to navigate. Those who can, employ the right people to navigate the tricky world of finance for them.

However, using the 4A Model of Marketing, Robinhood has broken down those barriers to show the rest of us how we can begin investing to earn money. Robinhood has done what the legendary Robin Hood did, with a twist. Give to the poor and the middle class what only the wealthy used to have access to.

Robinhood is a company that knows its target audience, and sets itself up immediately to accommodate its needs and desires. The world revolves around online commerce right now, and Robinhood has tapped into that. Clients can utilize their services through an app, a platform many of the younger generations are familiar and comfortable with using. In addition, the company has a substantial online presence, which makes it accessible to anyone with computer access.

Their website is to the point and concise, an approach that appeals to all customers. Their landing pages have a youthful feel, utilizing pictures that are not buffoonish in their cartoon-like nature, but contain an element of lightheartedness. There is a mixture of real-life images with drawings, and Robinhood combines these with eye-catching lines like "Join a new generation of investors." From links to cryptocurrency through the app, to an invitation to start building an investment portfolio for "just $1," Robinhood has made the financial world much easier to navigate for younger investors. Investment portfolios have always felt like they belong to individuals at the men's club establishments. A place in which many of us would not feel at ease. It's nice to see the rest of the population being offered opportunities for that economic potential.

## Pathos and Logos

Robinhood uses pathos and logos to convince potential clients that their investment firm is the one to use. Pathos, the appeal to emotions, is evident in their real-life images that show a younger generation of investors. When they address their message to the younger generation, it's almost a call to arms to join the elite few who have been investing and making money for generations. As if they are saying, "it's your turn, and it's easier than you believed" kind of thing. Logos, or the appeal to logic, is all over their website. They offer the research and the data you need to make an intelligent investment decision. Everything they offer has rates and statistics to utilize for decision-making. Unfortunately, Robinhood hasn't had many years in the investment firm market to back a claim of ethos or credibility. Therefore, they must rely on logos, the cold hard facts, to convince customers to join their team of investors.

## EDWARD JONES

Edward Jones is an investment firm with years of experience to back a claim of ethos or credibility. They have been on the "Fortune 500" list for ten consecutive years, giving them the biggest and best use of ethos a company could want. Edward Jones was established in 1922, 100 years ago. They add to their claim of ethos by establishing pathos—in 2017, when the CEO Action for Diversity and Inclusion launched, Edward Jones was one of the first companies to sign the pledge. Then, in 2019, Penny Pennington was named the firm's sixth managing partner. She was the only woman running a major U.S. brokerage firm. To add to the use of pathos, Edward Jones began as a family-owned and operated business when Edward Jones Sr.'s son, Ted, joined the firm in 1948. Combining pathos with ethos is an important marketing tool for any company, and Edward Jones does it well. However, in the case of an investment company, ethos is one of the key marketing strategies. When it comes to their money, clients want someone with a proven track record of navigating the world of investments.

After credibility comes the recognition that a company understands its target audience, and is willing to make some adjustments to service its needs. Edward Jones' website shows that they are still a powerhouse in the investment business. They are going to stick to the tried and true methods of service. Their website offers detailed information on how to begin an investment portfolio. They've included charts and links to pdf files to better understand what they'll do with your money. Then you're given a link to contact one of their financial advisors to get started.

However, this company has been around for 100 years, and they know a thing or two about investment companies. One of those things they know is how competitive the market is. To stay competitive today, especially against firms such as Robinhood, who have their finger on the pulse of the younger generation, the marketing strategies of Edward Jones have expanded to include online access to investing. It's not operated through an app, but it's a step in the right direction.

Edward Jones offers something else to their clients that goes toward logos. Clients recognize the logical side of doing business with their firm found in their paperwork. The company provides links to the financial reports required by the Securities and Exchange Act of 1934. Investing with a company that follows the rules, dots all the i's, and crosses all the t's is logical.

The investment firm of Edward Jones shows their clients that they understand the world's needs, and are willing to meet them. They have included a Sustainability Report and a Commitment to Inclusion, Diversity and Equity. As they say in their commitment, the company knows more work needs to be done. However, they are prepared and ready to embrace whatever it takes (Commitment to Inclusion, Diversity and Equity, n.d.).

In terms of transparency with their financial paperwork, and the sustainability and inclusion reports, Edward Jones addresses one of the 4As of Marketing: Acceptability. It is an essential component of the Marketing Mix, and Edward Jones meets both the functional and the psychological aspects of acceptability within marketing. Their company shows that the decision to become a client is functional; Edward Jones meets or exceeds the expectations of what an investment firm should be. Edward Jones also shows that investing with their firm is psychologically positive. Clients can feel comfortable knowing they're in good hands with a company that:

- Know what they're doing based on longevity and transparency with their financial reports
- Show they care about customers and the planet by putting together inclusion and sustainability reports.

The investment firms who have been around for a while know they must make some adjustments to continue servicing their clients, while increasing their client base.

# SCHWAB

Like any investment firm with longevity, Schwab also knows how to adjust its business practices to keep its existing clients while attracting new ones. Founded in 1971, the Charles Schwab Corporation has made it its goal to focus on the individual. Therefore, it has been a seamless process to accommodate the newer generations because, since 1975, every change the company implemented has benefited the investor. Schwab is one of those successful investment firms that understand that to keep their clients and gain new ones, they must keep moving forward with technology, and what the people want. As a result, they successfully 'read' the financial climate, and implement whatever changes are necessary, to stay on top.

## Accessibility

Schwab has met more than one of the As in the Marketing Mix. They have Accessibility covered, with existing clients receiving a monthly newsletter way back at the beginning. Allowing customers to know what's going on with their investment firm is a good way of keeping them involved in their investments and investing. So when the Internet reached the public in 1995, Schwab was ready to meet this new online world head-on. They had been preparing for this since 1975.

So Schwab activated their first website in 1995, right away making their investment company more accessible to the public, or at least to anyone who had access to the internet.

Schwab made a bold move with accessibility in 1982, offering 24/7 order entry and quote services. The company recognizes that people don't always have access during bankers' hours. This move puts accessibility front and center with the company. That accessibility increased when they began offering a mobile app for clients to do their investing with Schwab.

Schwab continued with accessibility when they recognized teenagers need to learn how to handle money. So in 2021, they began programs that support teen financial literacy. This is a move designed to make their investment firm and what they have to offer available to potential new clients.

## Affordability

It's not only accessibility that Schwab has mastered; they have also reached the Affordability goal in the Marketing Mix. Throughout the years, Schwab has interpreted people's financial needs, and implemented programs designed to make investing affordable. These moves allowed more people to invest than would typically be able to, meaning that their economic well-being did not have to be a hindrance. The following are some examples:

- 1992: adjusted mutual fund investing with no transaction fees
- 1996: low-cost online investing, which cuts the commission but benefits the client
- 2005: made banking simpler for investors—no more unnecessary costs
- 2009: because commissions can severely undermine an investment portfolio, Schwab made commission-free ETFs (exchange-traded funds)

- 2015: no fee investment advisory service
- 2019: Schwab made investment available to everyone, moving US stock, ETFs, and online trade commissions to $0

These are just a few of the programs Schwab implemented in their investment company, allowing more people to invest. From the beginning, Schwab's goal has been to help everyone, which shows in their marketing.

## Ethos, Logos, Pathos

Schwab also uses pathos, which is evident immediately when you reach their website. Their pictures show family members smiling; Schwab shows that investing can be suitable for the family, and they're tugging on the heartstrings to get this message across. Quotes are littered throughout the site as well, talking about families, and how the Schwab company puts its clients first.

Schwab, though, is a company that uses all three: pathos, logos, and ethos. Their use of pathos is evident in the paragraph above. We can also see how Schwab applies logos through their use of the 4As of Marketing. The programs and the changes they have made over the years prove that they are a logical choice when looking for the right investment firm. They know what people want, and they're willing and able to put that knowledge to good use. They are smart enough to be ahead of the game when implementing some of their programs, and everything proves that it works. They post numbers, and they have won awards; national, industry, and all others.

The same can be said for ethos. Schwab has a track record, and the awards and accolades prove that it's a working model that can and will benefit prospective investors.

Like most other investment firms, there are other marketing tools available, and Schwab uses them to their advantage.

- Research: Schwab does the research; then they show you the results
- Surveys: Schwab sends out surveys, and then lets you know what those surveys say
- Press Releases: Schwab makes the most of the press, and they aren't afraid to broadcast those newsworthy moments

Marketing is a valuable tool for any company, and these investment firms are smart enough to make good use of the marketing tools available. The fact that they are wise enough to market their firms as well as they do stands as testament to the ethos of all three of these companies discussed in this chapter.

# Chapter 2

# CRYPTOCURRENCY EXCHANGE COMPANIES

Cryptocurrency is something relatively new in the world of finance. To better explain, cryptocurrency is an electronic cash system not owned or processed by a bank. Instead, owning cryptocurrency means you don't hold tangible objects like a house, car, or money. It means you have a key that transfers information from one person to another without a third party. The transactions are supposed to be incredibly secure, so user identity is unknown. Therefore, you can send cryptocurrency anonymously. Coding technology keeps transactions and currencies safe. Experts believe investors will soon use cryptocurrency to trade bonds, stocks, and other assets.

That day may already be here. The cryptocurrency phase began in 2009 with Bitcoin, but has become a worldwide phenomenon. Multiple investment and financial institutions, such as the ones in this chapter, are already offering cryptocurrency services.

The use of cryptocurrency seems unreal because you're using money that doesn't exist in the real world. However, you're purchasing a very real form of currency, and it is very secure. According to Amanda Triest of startupnation.com, the security is due to a blockchain; a digital ledger used to list cryptocurrency transactions. Its security makes it impossible to counterfeit or double-spend the cryptocurrency. However, she also reminds us that there are Pros and Cons to investing in cryptocurrency:

## PROS

- No need for social security number or personal information when purchasing cryptocurrency
- No monthly fees
- Transactions are fast, taking minutes because they happen in real time
- No need to visit an ATM or a bank. Everything can be done from your phone or computer

## CONS

- Lose your key, lose your money—password keys are long and difficult to remember, and there's no password reset or help button.
- No insurance, so if you or your provider loses the money, it's gone
- Cannot dispute or reverse transactions
- The price fluctuates rapidly, and it can be tiresome to keep track of fluctuations

However, the cons don't outweigh the pros for many people, and the newer generations of investors are keen to utilize the online world of finance. Cryptocurrency is precisely that—online finance.

## BINANCE

Binance is a finance company that has been around since 2017, and specializes in cryptocurrency. Like almost all finance companies, it uses ethos and logos in marketing. Their website uses statistics and numbers to prove that they're knowledgeable about crypto, while promoting the logical argument that using their company for cryptocurrency transactions is the best way to go, because they know their stuff. The logic dictates that if a company is good at what they do, then it's inevitable that you will use their services.

Clients have a lot to learn when dealing with investing. Binance understands this and offers a "Learn and Earn" section. Once you've accessed this section, some links will take you to various parts of the website to study, then take a quiz to see how much you learned from the reading material. Cryptocurrency is a strange new world of finance, but its idea holds many more questions than answers. This classroom style of understanding cryptocurrency is an excellent marketing strategy for Binance. They understand what people need, and then give it to them. There are other ways this finance company markets its services:

## Digital Storytelling:

Digital storytelling is content on their website that educates, entertains, or helps the reader or customer. Binance's website educates the client. Their links to the classes to learn about the world of cryptocurrency are probably the best form of education. One cannot begin investing with cryptocurrency if one does not understand how it works. The classes offer this vital information to prospective clients, making it easier for them to decide to begin trading in crypto. The process is seamless, because once the customer has learned what they need to know, starting the process is just a click away.

## Self-Service and Digitalization

The newer generation of investors wants to do their work online. They would rather not go to a bank when it's easier and more convenient to do their banking from their phones. Binance, like all good finance companies, recognizes this and offers these investors what they need. What you get is convenient banking and investing on the go.

## Automation and Big Data

Finance companies know what areas of finance customers are most interested in, and which links are used most often on their web pages. The data allows companies like Binance to tailor their website to provide investors' wants.

Binance has used the marketing tools available to them, and put together a website that allows investors to begin the journey into cryptocurrency in a place where they're most comfortable. They can use the website and its tools at their convenience, and from the privacy of their own home, which allows companies like Binance to become successful and stay successful. But they don't leave it up to guesswork. Their website offers you the chance to fill out a survey, another marketing tool designed to help them keep their clients while gaining new ones.

# COINBASE

Coinbase has been around since 2012, and they are another finance company specializing in cryptocurrency. Coinbase markets its services using not only ethos and logos, but also pathos. For example, a page on its website introduces the executive team. Who wouldn't feel at home with a company that gives a title like "Chief People Officer" to one of their executives?

## Blog

Coinbase has a blog like many companies do today. Blogs are an excellent means of communication with customers; even finance companies like

Coinbase recognize their customers' desire to know what's going on. It's probably even more evident in the financial world, since money is the most critical commodity. An investor wants to ensure that the company that has their money also knows what they're doing, and a blog can answer many questions without the customer having to ask. Therefore, a blog is an essential marketing tool.

## Social Media

Not only do they use a blog as a marketing tool, but Coinbase also has a presence on many social media platforms. Twitter, Facebook, Instagram, YouTube, and LinkedIn are the ones listed on their website to follow. This marketing tool is essential in gaining new clients, while proving that their employees are people too. In addition, social media helps showcase the family side of a company.

Although new to the finance world compared to others, Coinbase utilizes the same marketing tools vital to any finance company's growth and stability. Its website is an easy-to-follow format that applies the following:

## Digital Storytelling

Coinbase's content is very informative and educational. They offer tools to teach prospective clients about cryptocurrency. Although it's not in the same lessons and quizzes format you find on Binance's website, the information is formatted well. They are called Beginner's Guides, and they are easy reads. At the end of each, the reader can read a guide that covers some key terms found within the beginner's guide they just read.

Coinbase also offers a guide to taxes on cryptocurrency. Within this guide, they are firm in their explanation that it is simply a guide to understanding the most basic tax information about cryptocurrency, information that will change each year. They strongly urge the reader to consult their tax accountant about the specifics. They just feel that the client needs to know what they're getting into regarding taxes.

One of the biggest perks to the education they offer clients is the Glossary. But unfortunately, cryptocurrency is like anything else in finance. It has a language that can make entering the cryptocurrency world highly confusing and scary.

## Self-Service and Digitization

Everything is self-service on the Coinbase website, as well. As a result of the newer generation looking to invest, this marketing tool has become the most popular among finance companies. Companies like Coinbase know their target audience well, and offer what the newer investors want: the ability to do their banking on their own terms, and in their own time.

## Automation and Big Data

It's a given that all finance companies will have automation and big data embedded into their websites. There's no chance to succeed and prosper if they don't know what potential investors are looking for, and not everyone is the same. Therefore, they must be ready to offer all services that will account for every type of investor. Although Coinbase provides most of the same benefits that companies like Binance do, there are tiny differences such as the Tax information and the Glossary. It's these little touches that set each company apart from the rest. But of course, it also makes choosing the right finance company a little more difficult for the investor.

## Social Media

Social media is a platform that all companies want to use to their advantage. So although I haven't mentioned it as a marketing tool in the above companies, it's a given that it will be in one way or another, especially for finance companies striving to boost their client base. Most finance companies that have been around long before social media have taken a little longer to embrace its possibilities as a marketing tool. However, companies like Binance and Coinbase are newer, and recognize the power a social media platform offers. In the upcoming chapters of this book, I will talk about how companies can use social media for more than just advertising. It is also closely linked to more marketing tools such as Influencers.

# ETORO

eToro is another newer company. It started in 2007 with a slightly different take on investing. This company calls what they do social investing, or social investment networks. eToro is not a company that specializes in cryptocurrency. The company didn't add that feature to its services until 2018. Mobile apps weren't part of their investment services until 2012.

But eToro's approach is a little different with some identical features. They also have learning tools for learning cryptocurrency, called eToro's Online Trading Academy. So again, there are classes, but they're for both new and seasoned investors. Another feature eToro offers its investors is a nod to the newer generation of fledgling investors. They call it the Copy Trader, and it started in 2010.

Copy Trader helps the new customers who want to invest like the seasoned pros but cannot afford the fees. So eToro offered a new service that allows clients to directly copy the investments of top traders—with no cost. This feature can act both as a learning tool and a cost-saving tool.

eToro has a page of reviews, another marketing tool. These reviews are sometimes the final push for new clients to get them to sign up with a program, and are excellent marketing tools.

As with the rest of the finance companies, eToro uses ethos and logos as practical marketing tools. However, the term "social investment networks" seems confusing initially, because investing is a one-person deal. But as you move through the website, it begins to make sense. eToro is also heavily involved with social media platforms, the same ones Coinbase is:

- Facebook
- Twitter
- Instagram
- YouTube
- LinkedIn

However, they have added a social media platform exclusive to eToro, which makes the company showcase its use of pathos as a marketing tool. It is such a familiar tactic that it makes the company seem likable and like one big family. They also treat their customers like family when using this tool.

eToro considers itself more than just a company; it is a community. They have a news feed that acts as their own social media platform. eToro customers can interact with one another, posting updates and commenting on others' posts like any other social media site. However, there is an additional feature.

Customers can share their portfolios, hoping to have them copied, which brings in a slight gain through eToro's Popular Investor Program. It sounds like having your portfolio copied is on the same level as getting 'likes' on Facebook or Instagram.

eToro is showing longevity in the world of finance, and it is evident they follow the same marketing tactics as the rest. They also use:

- Digital Storytelling: The story eToro is telling starts with a video. It's a short, 51-second ad that promotes eToro. Admittedly, the customers featured are younger than you'd expect from an investment firm, but that's the point, isn't it? After all, the ad highlights using a mobile app to invest with eToro.
- Self-Service and Digitization: A mobile app is a form of self-service. Of course, as with all financial institutions today, banking with eToro includes the ability to access your account online.

Across the globe, banking has become digitized, and it would be rare to find a financial company that has not embraced this portion of the digital world.

- Automation and Big Data: The website allows customers to begin investing with the click of a button. One of the most appealing features to younger investors today is that they don't have to spend time in a bank. Instead, they can accomplish everything they want online, or through a mobile app. Of course, they don't mind asking questions when necessary, but they also know their capabilities. Let's remember that many of these younger investors were helping us set up their cell phones, or navigating the internet, when they were ten.

- Social Media: To get their name in front of a new generation of investors, financial companies need to promote themselves through social media platforms. Since this type of business is constantly aware of necessary adaptations, the move to advertising through Facebook or YouTube is a no-brainer.

Financial companies sometimes require different marketing tools because they sell a service rather than a product. However, your service is a product of you, so the same marketing techniques should and do apply to both.

# Chapter 3

# FINANCIAL HOLDING COMPANIES

Financial holding companies is a fancy term for banks. Although banks hold your money, they are in business to make money. Therefore, they must use many of the same marketing tools used by investment firms and other financial companies. The banks in this chapter are some of the most successful, and have been around for many years. Their marketing strategies are tried-and-true, and have proven to work. It's not unusual to encounter a bank that used to have another name until a more significant bank purchased them—a standard process with banks. The first bank in this chapter is an example of one that had one or more predecessors before becoming the bank it is today.

## JP MORGAN CHASE & CO. (JPM)

JP Morgan Chase & Co. began in 1799 as The Bank of the Manhattan Company, and the bank's long history can be a marketing tool. The website offers a timeline where JP Morgan has the opportunity to name-drop. Reading the timeline might be a glimpse into the oldest form of celebrity endorsement. JP Morgan uses influencers such as Alexander Hamilton, Aaron Burr, and Abraham Lincoln to extol its virtues.

## Ethos, Logos, Pathos

But the most significant portion of the bank's marketing strategy is its use of ethos, logos, and pathos. JP Morgan has combined all three. The bank's history is the first to utilize ethos and logos, because it highlights why this bank is so good at what it does. There are excellent reasons behind each merger or acquisition since 1799 to bring them where they are today.

However, the appeal to emotions, or pathos, is tremendous for JP Morgan. The bank has artfully woven the marketing strategy of Customer Outreach, with pathos, then added a sprinkle of Digital Storytelling to pull it all together. As a result, everything you read on their website is an emotional reason to use JP Morgan Chase & Co. for your banking needs. This bank shows that it has nothing but the best in mind for the entire planet!

Then the website proves that not only do they have these beautiful ideas, but they actually implement them daily. The following marketing strategies are crucial to promoting JP Morgan & Chase Co. as the bank to do business with:

## Digital Storytelling

The website reads like a picture storybook. Yes, there are pictures, and they tell their own story. But, for some, the image is the appeal. JP Morgan is a master at digital storytelling, and everything you read makes the company look amazing.

## Customer Outreach

We have not addressed Customer Outreach as a marketing tool, but JP Morgan is excellent at utilizing this tactic. The company brings awareness to underserved communities, which shows they care. It's a great tool to show that if they care about everybody, even those who don't bank with them, they will care about someone who uses their services.

## Public Relations

A large portion of the website is devoted to expressing this marketing tactic. JP Morgan deftly uses the media to prove their involvement in community projects by expanding on the customer outreach tactic. The media can be a valuable tool in promoting a business; JP Morgan seems to know how to use that part of the marketing system.

## Events

There are several events that JP Morgan has sponsored or held, but the first one shown is titled "Bringing Art to the People in Richmond," and it is one of the links in which the picture is the first draw. The event involves an "artmobile," a mobile art museum in an expandable trailer. It's just one of the ways JP Morgan uses a marketing strategy that shows a bank's human side, while making it seem appealing.

# BANK OF AMERICA

The original banking institution of this next financial holding company was formed in 1904 by Amadeo Peter Giannini. After an acquisition in 1998, it became the Bank of America, now the second largest bank after JP Morgan. In an interesting turn of phrase, its website explicitly states that the oldest parts of this bank go back 204 years, but I cannot find anything to verify this information. Therefore, we will use the 1904 date to be as accurate as possible.

## Pathos

Bank of America is another financial institution that uses ethos, logos, and pathos. I imagine many people would be surprised to find pathos, the appeal to emotion, as a marketing tool for a bank. However, these larger banks have recognized the need to be viewed as human rather than cold, lifeless automatons. After all, it's a sense of family that brings in customers.

Pathos is an effective marketing tool for Bank of America through pictures of families,  and the use of that marketing strategy utilized by financial institutions:

## Customer Outreach

Bank of America shows its Customer Outreach differently than JP Morgan, but it's just as effective. For example, the bank's diversity statement and policy state more than once that Bank of America would not be where it is without its customers, and the company values teamwork with those customers. Bank of America also has a sustainability program on its web page. Both show that Bank of America values the community, and cares about the world's future for future generations. The company also focuses on the present; they offer initiatives to provide health care to underserved communities.

## Surveys

Bank of America asks that customers fill out surveys, a marketing tool that allows companies to adjust their services to help where there are gaps.

## Press Releases

Like JP Morgan and the rest, Bank of America also uses the media to promote its customer outreach, and the statistics that make it worth being a bank member. While some might view their press releases as a bit of bragging, when choosing the right bank to protect your money, every piece of information is necessary.

Like JP Morgan and many large banks, Bank of America uses other, familiar marketing strategies. Among them are:

- Digital Storytelling—although not on the same level as JP Morgan, all the information on the website is a story worth being told.
- Self-Service and Digitization—Bank of America is no different from the rest; they recognize the need for mobile apps, and a complete do-it-yourself banking package.
- Automation and Big Data—Links on the website gather the necessary information Bank of America needs to streamline its customers' services.

Although the strategies used by banking institutions are generally the same, there are always a few minor differences. It sets each bank apart; each is looking to attract new customers, and the data they collect might show enough of a difference on their web pages. However, the location of the main branch will be another factor in a customer's decision to sign on with the financial institution.

# CITIGROUP

Citigroup began in 1811, called the National City Bank of New York. Then, after another name change and a merger, it became Citigroup. Just 12 years younger than JP Morgan, Citigroup takes advantage of the same marketing strategies. Based on this bank's longevity, these tactics are successful.

## Ethos and Logos

Citigroup relies on logos and ethos, with little to no pathos involved. Yes, they have a diversity and sustainability program, but this bank takes a more statistical track for its marketing. It is a bank, after all, and based on the history they offer, they have made the company succeed based on the numbers. Ethos and logos work very well for Citibank; it still manages to come across as a friendly company. Of course, a picture of a smiling employee helps to promote that opinion.

Citigroup does rely on marketing strategies that help tone down the logical side of its website presentation. For example, it offers:

## Blog

No matter what, a blog lends a friendly tone to any website. When a company takes the time to write about community outreach programs, diversity and equity programs, and sustainability issues, the company cares. Everything comes across in a soothing tone; the colors are correct, and the language is excellent. None of it sounds like forced ideas or empty promises. Instead, it sounds like a company that recognizes they have the power to do something, and are willing to take the appropriate steps.

## Press Releases

Like all banking institutions, press releases offer the community access to the company's good deeds. I cannot say it enough; this is a good thing. Therefore, with their lack of pathos, the press releases give the sense of family that is missing from the webpage.

Citigroup also uses other standard marketing strategies:

- Self-Service and Digitization: Once the customers are drawn in through the company's deft use of the numbers to state their case, they know their clients will still want to do their banking their way. I think this marketing tool is here to stay with banks.
- Automation and Big Data: Companies that provide a service, especially money-managing or investments, must use Big Data to track what their customers want. All companies should use it, but financial institutions are in a trickier business. When it comes to someone else's money, you've got to get it right.
- Digital Storytelling: Citibank doesn't rely much on digital storytelling, but there is some. When you think about it, any

business with an online presence utilizes digital storytelling to some degree.

- Customer Outreach: Citibank, like all financial institutions, recognizes the value of helping the community.

Citigroup does not push the customer outreach to the front, but it is there. It's almost as though it's woven into a tapestry, the shiny gold threads among the muted colors. And honestly, that makes for a relaxing read.

# NAVY FEDERAL CREDIT UNION

Credit unions are banking institutions but with a smaller target audience. A credit union is exclusive, in that customers are limited to a specific group of people. In the case of the Navy Federal Credit Union, a customer must be an active or former member of the armed forces. Inclusion is extended to family members, as well. With this narrow target audience in mind, let's take a look at this particular credit union's marketing strategies.

First, Navy Federal Credit Union was established in 1933 with branches in 30 states. Generally, a credit union that services the armed forces is found on military bases. Credit unions like this one can be found in other countries as well. This is a benefit of a credit union that caters to the military. See a need, fill a need.

Because credit unions do not offer their banking services to just anyone, its marketing strategies are geared toward one group, which means the tools used are limited as well, or at least not as broad in scope. However, because Navy Federal is a banking institution, and its customer base is military with sometimes odd hours and locations, some marketing strategies are the same as other banks.

## Accessibility

Because it services active duty service members, Navy Federal Credit Union offers online banking, branches in other countries, and a mobile app. Military members find themselves in other countries, or working odd hours with limited access to banking, so being able to do all their banking online is a big perk of banking with this credit union. There are ATMs available, as well. Just because it's not a huge corporation does not mean it doesn't offer all the banking amenities a company like JP Morgan gives.

## Engagement

Live chats are available on the website. Communicating through something called e-message through the website dashboard is also an option.

## Member-owned

One of the biggest attractions of using a credit union instead of a bank is that it's member-owned, and usually a not-for-profit company. Therefore, a credit union is able to offer lower loan rates, lower fees, and discounts offered exclusively to members.

## Code of Ethics

Navy Federal Credit Union has a strong code of ethics, and it puts customers first. This gives the company an edge in the marketing department. I have already stated, and I'll keep saying it; when a customer feels that the company cares, the customer will continue to give their business to that company.

## Ethos

Like all good banking institutions, Navy Federal offers reasons why a customer should find their services credible. From in-house experts to awards and recognitions, it's all on these websites for customers to peruse.

# Chapter 4

# BUSINESS MARKETING CONSULTANT FIRMS

L ike a bank, business marketing consultant firms help other companies make money. But they have to make money as well. So they must market their services to gain more clients, to pay them for helping them make more money. What a circle! These business marketing consultant firms should know the most about marketing strategies, and how to apply them to other people's businesses, let alone their own. So let's see what they have to offer.

## IBM BUSINESS CONSULTING

IBM is a big name, one that has been around for years. It is a global company and one that knows how to make money. Therefore, the idea that it now offers business consulting seems like a natural extension of their skills.

It's more than just the marketing that IBM Consulting provides. The background of IBM proves that they are the ones to turn to when it comes to any aspect of a business, and marketing is just a tiny portion of it. IBM Consulting focuses on ethos and logos to get its point across, and there is not much room for pathos. Their sales pitch does not indicate any appeal to emotion.

But IBM Consulting does not need to appeal to emotions for their services. They are strictly a technology-based company, and their services reflect that.

It makes sense that IBM Consulting would capitalize on its experience in the technical side of the business. However, that logic extends to the idea that if they're so good at building the technical side of a company, it makes sense that they would understand every facet of the business world. They've been doing it for decades.

IBM launched in 1911 from the merger of three companies in business since the late 1800s. So you could say that IBM has been around since the late 1800s. The company is responsible for many core technologies that made computers a staple in the business world. Their track record speaks for itself, which makes this company more than qualified to offer business consulting.

Although they are no longer at the forefront of creating new technologies, they still invest heavily in the industry. The history of this company is part of its marketing strategy. You cannot deny their expertise runs deep; IBM invented many core technologies that run our computers, and even the internet today. But besides its history, IBM uses many of the same marketing strategies used by financial institutions.

For example:

## Digital Storytelling

It's all over the website. The story of what IBM does, how they do it, and how they can help your business do it. The story is told through statistics, charts, graphs, and images.

## Blogs

Like all good marketing strategies, IBM utilizes a blog to tell its story. It's a personal way to connect with customers, and newcomers to their website. Spending time on a business's website is great, but reading the blog offers a one-on-one connection. The blog is probably the only place you will get a sense of pathos, and it isn't necessarily in the stories told on the blog. Just the fact that there is a blog that the company has taken the time to offer foreshadows the rest that they will do for you.

## Automation and Big Data

IBM is a company that has specialized in computer technologies, and the technical aspects of all businesses, for decades. So you can bet the company will utilize the automation and big data aspect of marketing. It's just simply what they do.

Not all marketing consulting firms work the same, and all don't come from the purely technical side that IBM does. However, they all use the same marketing tools, although they may be applied differently. Therefore, IBM is an excellent example of how a company uses the same marketing tools differently.

# ILLUMINATION CONSULTING

A newer company, Illumination Consulting, began in 1998. Their website is full of marketing tactics, which makes sense. That's what the company does; they show businesses how to market themselves to grow successfully. And what better way to prove they know what they're doing, than by putting their tools to work for them on their website. There is a long list of the marketing strategies Illumination Consulting uses.

## Digital Storytelling

The story of Illumination Consulting is well-told. The company spells it out clearly on its website. While reading, you can see every bit of the marketing tools companies use to sell their services. Because, like financial institutions, these marketing companies sell a service rather than a product.

## Social Media

Illumination Consulting doesn't miss a beat, especially with its presence on social media platforms. They've got them all covered:

- Facebook
- Twitter
- Tumblr
- YouTube
- LinkedIn
- Pinterest
- Instagram

## Engagement

One form of engagement is a marketing tool that is front and center, quickly noticed when you reach the website. On the bottom right of your screen, you'll see a tab with the words "Chat with us," and a waving hand. Rather than trying to navigate the whole website to find what you're looking for, Illumination hopes you'll click on that, and begin a live chat. This chat is how the company builds rapport with prospective and existing customers.

## Self-Service and Digitization

The self-service portion of marketing doesn't work the best with a marketing company; this is a tool that financial institutions implement to give customers the ability to handle their money, without having to go to a bank. However, the bit of interaction found within the website offers solace to the customers who want to do as much as they can themselves. There are opportunities to click and learn more; this is the closest to a self-service you'll get here. But it allows prospective customers to get an accurate picture of what Illumination can do, allowing them to decide if using this company's services is worthwhile. Customers today prefer to do their own research. Therefore, the few links enable the customer to do just that. These links are a form of accessibility, as well. The company makes the information accessible to the customer rather than expecting them to go into the business's office to make their decision.

## Email

Communicating by email generates leads for the business, and Illumination uses this wisely. There are several opportunities to enter your information to be contacted via email while searching the website. This tool works well for companies that offer a service or product that might be costly, giving potential customers time to decide, while allowing the company to provide more incentives or information, whichever the customer needs.

Newsletters can be thrown into this marketing strategy, as well. Offering a potential or existing customer the chance to sign up for a newsletter allows a company like Illumination to provide more information to that customer. The newsletter either encourages the existing customer that they've made the right choice, or gives the prospective customer the chance to see what they could be a part of if they chose to use the company's services.

## Blog

I have already said a lot about using a blog as a marketing strategy, but it is an effective tool. A lot of time and effort goes into creating a blog, and the company that invests this time into one shows that they would also be willing to invest that kind of time and effort into their customers. So, if you want to keep existing customers while getting new ones, post a blog and show them you care.

## Testimonials

Nothing advertises a company's worth more than word of mouth. Testimonials are an excellent marketing tool. It's typical for people to buy something because a friend told them it's a fantastic product. We all want what everyone else has, don't we? So let others sell your business!

## Ethos and Logos

I can't stress enough how every company uses one or more of these three tools to market their business. While pathos is not an overt part of the Illumination marketing strategy, ethos and logos are compelling enough without it. Illumination uses logos in the statistics they post on their website. They use ethos through testimonials, and the information they give about what they will do to build a company. A company simply cannot successfully market itself without at least one of these tools.

# IGNITE VISIBILITY

Ignite Visibility begins its marketing strategy with the name of the company. Like some of the other companies mentioned in this book, the company's name can be a marketing strategy. Maybe the company name has been around for decades. Or it might be because the company created something life-changing. Whatever the reason, the name can be a very effective marketing tool. This company's name sparks a picture in your mind. See what I did there? Sparks is another word for ignite. Sparks will ignite a fire, and to start a fire…well, I'm sure you get where

I'm going. This company is letting you know they will show you how to create a fire that will make your company visible.

Ignite Visibility has been around since 2013. When you reach the website, you get a taste of the Ethos used as a marketing tool. Ignite Visibility's credibility is front and center with its list of awards. This credibility continues throughout the page. Their credibility increases when you realize they have created a proprietary digital marketing forecast system.

Then there's logos, when the website begins citing numbers and statistics. Beyond that, Ignite Visibility uses the rest of the tools slightly differently from the other companies we've discussed so far.

## Blog

Not only does Ignite Visibility have a blog, but they also have a newsletter. However, they've gone a step better with videos and podcasts. Though newer than the others, this company has embraced its target audience. Ignite Visibility realizes that younger generations are starting businesses, and they know what these entrepreneurs want. It's a big step for many customers to use social media platforms in their marketing. Every once in a while, you get a company that knows that social media extends farther than the standard platforms like Facebook and Instagram. Podcasts are the future. I know many young people would rather listen to a podcast than read a book, or watch tv.

## Social Media

As with any younger business, Ignite Visibility has embraced social media platforms. It's a great tool; if you're going to reach the younger business owners, go where you know they'll be, and that is social media. Even a brief presence on any social media site will gain the notice a company like Ignite needs.

## Testimonials

Ignite Visibility puts some of their testimonials right on the main page of their website. There is a particular page to read them in-depth, but a prospective customer immediately sees what Ignite means to its existing customers. I view this as an excellent strategy because, as I've mentioned before, a business owner wants to know if they're researching a company that has received good reviews. Again, we all want what others have.

## Case Studies

Case studies as a marketing tool are another area in which Ignite Visibility stands out from the rest. Ignite Visibility publishes the studies with the questions and answers they sent to existing customers. They don't just pick and choose the answers they want to highlight on their website; they show the whole thing.

## Pathos

Even though Ignite Visibility is a business marketing company, it utilizes pathos much more than other companies do. Its website shows an evident diversity and inclusion statement, program, and a solid commitment to serving the community.

Studying the marketing techniques of companies in the financial world that sell themselves as products has been enlightening. Let's see how they compare to different types of companies. Let's look at how much is the same, and what is different.

# Chapter 5

---

# WEIGHT LOSS PROGRAMS

I can't think of a better marketing tool for testimonials than weight loss companies. Weight loss companies work because someone tries their program, and it works for them. Then they tell all their friends about it, and next thing you know, the company has gained more clients. The best testimonial for any company is that their product or program worked, and benefited someone. Many weight loss companies also use celebrity endorsements as an effective marketing tool. For example, if you're watching television and an actor loses weight, your first thought is that they have a personal trainer. However, if you find out they lost weight because of a weight loss company, you will want to try the same program. Because, hey, you can afford the weight loss program, while a personal trainer may be out of the question.

There are several different types of weight loss programs today. So I've tried to break them into categories for each chapter. This one, Chapter 5, will focus on a few general weight loss programs. Chapter 6 is about weight loss programs that are strictly online, from their apps to their interactions with the company. Chapter 7 is about weight loss programs with specially designed meal kits. Finally, Chapter 8 is all about weight loss programs designed for more than just weight loss; it's a package of health and skincare.

# WEIGHTWATCHERS

Weight Watchers was founded in 1963, giving them years to perfect their marketing strategies. The top two tactics this company uses are the following:

## Testimonials

Losing weight is one of the most challenging things to do, and for many people, whatever program worked for someone else is the one they want to try. Testimonials will be a marketing tool used by every weight loss company in the following chapters, but it's interesting to see how each company handles or presents them.  When you get to the Weight Watchers website, testimonials are the first things you see. They take up most of the main page. Of course, the testimonials are on almost every page as you navigate the website. So naturally, this form of marketing is the number one choice for a weight loss company. When you see someone who looks like you in their before picture, it's much easier to imagine your own body in their after photo.

## Celebrity Endorsements

You don't have to go far to see the celebrity endorsements for Weight Watchers. Since Lynn Redgrave in 1984, celebrities have been endorsing this long-lasting weight loss program. The celebrities who have endorsed the program also used it to lose weight. There are quite a few:

- Oprah: We have watched Oprah's weight fluctuate for years. Honestly, it's refreshing to know that someone famous has the same problems the rest of us do. As a Weight Watchers spokesperson, she did a lot of good for the company.
- Jessica Simpson
- Jennifer Hudson

- James Corden: Yes, even men need a weight loss program sometimes. Weight loss is not exclusive to women, and it is empowering for all genders that Weight Watchers proves this.
- Ciara
- Kate Hudson: This celebrity has never looked like she needed to lose weight. However, she is one of the many celebrities who has stated that while she only needed to lose 10 pounds, learning to eat healthily was the biggest and most crucial takeaway from this program.
- Tina Fey: Here is another celebrity who was never a spokesperson for Weight Watchers but was thankful she learned healthy eating habits during her time in the program.
- Jenny McCarthy
- Robbie Williams
- Daphne Oz
- Charles Barkley
- Sarah Ferguson
- Lynn Redgrave

We can see that celebrity endorsements can be helpful, and it doesn't always have to be about losing weight. However, the healthy eating habits these celebrities learned from this program are the best testimonials to the rest of us trying to figure out how to drop a few pounds.

## Accessibility

Let's go back to the 4 A's of marketing we mentioned in the first chapter. Weight Watchers uses a couple of those A's, as well. Accessibility is the first and foremost one seen in their marketing strategies. This weight loss program is available on a desktop or a mobile app. The customer can choose face-to-face interactions with coaches, or they can choose to do it all online. Whatever works for the customer makes the program accessible to everyone, no matter their preference.

So often, people say they just don't know what to eat when trying to lose weight. Weight Watchers offers a point system determined by your answers to their questions when you sign up. Foods are designated points, and you plan your meals based on the number of points you have for the day and what each food is worth. Additionally, the exercise you do each day can adjust your points. For some, knowing which foods are the best to eat doesn't always help because they don't know what to make with them. Weight Watchers offers recipes to solve this problem.

Each of these comes down to accessibility. Is this something a customer can do? Weight Watchers tries to make the weight loss journey as pain-free as possible. Along with accessibility comes:

## Affordability

It's normal; weight loss programs are going to cost. That price, though, can be a heavy burden on many people, making the idea of losing weight something to put aside until they have a little extra money. However, Weight Watchers has specials all the time. You can't miss these special deals; they're just a click away every few scrolls down the page. Almost every section leads to signing up and taking advantage of the discounts offered.

## Ethos and Pathos

The longevity of this company is part of what leads to the ethos portion of marketing. In addition, the testimonials and celebrity endorsements show Weight Watchers' credibility regarding weight loss.

So, how does pathos fit? Well, every testimonial is a story that reaches out to families and people who need to lose weight, whether it's to fit into clothes they haven't worn in years, or to solve a health issue due to excess weight. Whatever it is, pathos appeals to emotions, and weight loss is an appeal to emotions.

Now let's see what other weight loss programs have for their marketing strategies.

# TRIM DOWN CLUB

The Trim Down Club began in 2012. It doesn't have the longevity that Weight Watchers does, but it focuses on almost the same things. For example, testimonials are the main focus when you reach the website. Again, this is common for weight loss programs. What is the point in trying a weight loss program if it doesn't work for anyone else?

Although the marketing strategies are generally the same, their structure may differ.

## Surveys

For instance, the Trim Down Club has a Survey button that pops up as soon as you enter the website. Surveys are an essential marketing tool, especially for a company as young as the Trim Down Club. While the founders may have been a team of specialists, specifically dietitians and nutritionists, that doesn't mean they are experts in marketing. However, they recognize the tools to help them with that, and asking people to fill out surveys is one way to accomplish that goal. Surveys need to be filled out by more than the people who join. Seriously, the company needs to know what people think of their website, what interested them, and what made them say no to the program.

## Ethos

Talking about the team of experts in the field of health and weight loss, that piece of information right there backs the claim to credibility or ethos. Knowing experts designed the program helps you decide to join a weight loss program. Again, weight loss is so tricky for everyone to navigate that it's reassuring that the person in charge is knowledgeable.

The Tips and Tricks section of the website also goes toward the program's credibility. Through this bit, the Trim Down Club offers advice on everything from losing weight with menopause, to choosing the right foods for diabetes. Then there are the following:

## Accessibility

The Trim Down Club understands the need for accessibility within their program. They also offer recipes and a mobile app for those who want a complete online experience. It seems that weight loss programs are understanding their target audiences, and recognizing the need to take full advantage of the services, without the inconvenience of attending meetings or picking up products from a warehouse or office space. These weight loss programs left the original program style behind. They have progressed to what people want now.

## Social Media

Like any successful company today, the Trim Down Club is ready to take full advantage of social media platforms. People post everything on their social media accounts, from what they just ate to the book they're reading. So why not allow them to share the weight loss program they're using? Not only does it satisfy the customer's need to share everything in their life, it also gives the Trim Down Club exposure to potential customers.

## Engagement

The Trim Down Club has a unique way of engaging with its customers through the website. According to their information, they view their customers as part of a community. So, why not take the idea of community to the next level? They offer a Live Forum where customers can chat about their weight loss journey. It's an excellent marketing and motivational tool for a weight loss program. While people are content to take this journey on their own with just an online presence, it still helps to know there are others out there experiencing the same things you are. The forum gives members a chance to share their struggles, their questions, and their successes.

## Pathos

Like Weight Watchers, Trim Down uses pathos as a marketing tool. Losing weight is an emotional journey, and every testimony proves it. The theme behind the Trim Down Club also shows customers' emotional journey when they join this weight loss program. The idea is in the name—of a club, a community for like-minded individuals traveling the road of weight loss together, sharing the ups and downs of losing weight. That suggests you're a family member once you join. You are, again, speaking to the emotional connection that is pathos.

# MAYO CLINIC DIET

While the Mayo Clinic has been around for over 100 years, the Mayo Clinic Diet was started in 2010, making it a pretty young weight loss program. Based on its name, the first page of the website is devoted almost entirely to ethos as a marketing tool, showcasing the reasons this program is credible. The weight loss program is built entirely around health, and changing the way you eat versus a fad diet. The website's main page expands on this idea in bits and pieces.

## Testimonials

The Mayo Clinic Diet's webpage does touch on testimonials as a marketing tool. However, they are not front and center like the other two weight loss programs discussed in this chapter. Instead, a small section is devoted to it midway through the main page, which is too easy to miss.

The rest have to be searched out, and they're called Success Stories. Some marketing tactics are the same as the other programs, though. These include the following:

## Engagement

A chat box on the website's main page offers the opportunity to interact and ask questions. The Mayo Clinic Diet program also indicates there is a new feature that is available in 2022; virtual group video sessions with Mayo Clinic doctors for customers interested in a healthy lifestyle versus a fad diet. Yes, there are testimonials to prove that the program works, but for some, the fact that doctors from such a renowned medical facility are involved makes this program easily the best one to follow.

## Blogs

The Mayo Clinic Diet program does have a blog. No matter how clinical the program may feel to some, there still has to be that feeling of belonging. You get that feeling of community through a blog, and the program loses some of the clinical feel.

## Social Media

Like the rest, the Mayo Clinic Diet recognizes the need to market its services through social media platforms.

## Accessibility

There is also a mobile app available for this weight loss program. Recipes and sample meal plans are also made available, although the recipes are only accessible to those who join the program. This is slightly different from the other weight loss programs, whose recipes are available to anyone visiting their site. However, the Mayo Clinic Diet program feels a little exclusive, which is a bonus for the customers who want that special feeling of belonging to a select group. Anyone searching the website can get a few recipes from the sample menu plans, but the casual observer cannot find their whole repertoire without first joining the club.

## Affordability

The plans for joining the Mayo Clinic Diet weight loss program are clearly laid out on the pricing page. They offer a couple of options to pay: in advance, or monthly. The programs are higher priced than Weight Watchers or the Trim Down Club, but still affordable if you consider how little you're paying in the end when you pay in advance.

There are many other weight loss programs, and the marketing strategies will be similar to the three in this chapter. However, how the company presents the tactics can be very different. As we have seen with the Mayo Clinic Diet, a company may prioritize different aspects of marketing.

# Chapter 6

---

# WEIGHT LOSS COMPANIES-ONLINE

Unsurprisingly, weight loss companies have begun focusing entirely on an online presence. The world has changed; weight loss programs must change to be effective. This chapter will discuss options for a client to lose weight using an online company, with no one-on-one interaction. Online capabilities give the client more control over their weight loss program, since they can work on it in their own home without traveling to pick up meals or supplements—a bonus for the busy person. Yes, these same benefits have been added to some of the more traditional weight loss programs, but the programs discussed in this chapter are much younger. Therefore, the online presence is the only way these programs have ever been intended to operate.

## PERFECT BODY

Perfect Body is an online weight loss program that began in 2020. A branch of Perfect Wellness Solutions, Perfect Body is the online answer to health clubs and gyms closed during the COVID quarantine. The name alone is a marketing tool, giving customers the idea that following this weight loss program could give them the perfect body they're looking for. Once customers are drawn in by the name, the rest of the marketing tools fall into place.

## Accessibility

Accessibility is the number one marketing tool this weight loss program utilizes. During the COVID quarantine, gyms and health clubs were closed, making online programs a desirable and sometimes necessary option for most of the population stuck at home. However, for the customer just looking, the website is not as full of information as the other weight loss programs. To see the program, you must answer their questions, then join. However, the bar at the bottom of the page offers tabs to read up on their policies.

## Testimonials

There are testimonials on the webpage, and they're called Reviews. Even though the website is not as open to non-members, the marketing strategy of drawing in new customers from testimonials is vital. Therefore, it's accessible to everyone.

## Ethos

Since the specific details, such as recipes, are not available to anyone trying to view the website for the Perfect Body weight loss program, the marketing strategy relied upon the most is Ethos. Offering as much statistics and pertinent information is the best they can do, unless you become a member.

The Perfect Body website is a no-nonsense approach to a weight loss system. Because it's online only, there is no paperwork. Everything is digital. Access to meal plans or pricing takes place only after you've joined, and there are quite a few questions to answer.

This online, no-fuss approach to a weight loss program is streamlined, and avoids clutter and confusion on a webpage. This is another form of accessibility, a marketing tool that works for the Perfect Body online community.

Let's see how many more online-based weight loss programs are the same.

# PLATEJOY

The PlateJoy weight loss program is another relatively new online presence. Established in 2013, the company feels less like a weight loss program, and more like a grocery program, except that it is a weight loss, healthy eating program. Like the others, PlateJoy offers its members a meal plan, using the point system as Weight Watchers does.

After perusing Perfect Body and PlateJoy, it emerges that one of the marketing strategies used by these online-based weight loss programs is a cleaner, less cluttered website. I would call this particular style part of the 4 As of Marketing.

## Accessibility

Besides offering its weight loss program online, which allows members to primarily use a mobile app, keeping a streamlined, clean website makes the program easier to access. Less maintenance on a website means more time spent on the program members. This marketing strategy is a win-win in two areas. One, prospective members don't need to wade through page after page of information to figure out how to join the program. Two, everything the members need is on the mobile app, so once they've joined, chances are they won't be revisiting the website. After all, the following marketing strategy will attract new members.

## Testimonials

PlateJoy does offer testimonials. Remember, it's a standard for all weight loss programs, even if they're online-based. There are not many on the website's main page, but each one covers a multitude of reasons why someone would use a weight loss program in the first place. From after-pregnancy weight loss to reducing food waste, any reason a prospective member would want to sign up with PlateJoy is covered in those testimonials.

PlateJoy has a tagline that makes a lot of sense, especially after seeing what they offer with their program. The slogan is "Healthy Eating for Busy People," and their services cover that exactly. But some of what the company provides makes them stand out from the others—another strategic marketing tactic. Use what the rest have but give it a little twist.

For example, the PlateJoy online weight loss program offers

- Grocery lists: they correlate to your personalized weekly menu. Therefore, there are no added expenses when you shop for groceries and no food you don't need.
- Optional grocery delivery: as a member, you can order your groceries online or use the mobile list mentioned above that matches your meal plan.

Based on the testimonials, this company almost literally takes the thinking out of meal planning for the busy customer. This is one of the biggest perks of signing up with this program.

PlateJoy's optimal plan for its members is to lose weight, and spend less on groceries with less waste. Fortunately, that plan might just go toward another marketing tool: pathos or the appeal to emotions. PlateJoy doesn't just care about the customer paying to sign up for their program. They care about the planet, food waste, and money wasted on unnecessary groceries. In essence, the company cares about the customer.

# NOOM

Noom is a little different from the rest of the weight loss programs. The company was founded in 2008, although the mobile app didn't launch until 2016. Noom takes a wildly different approach to weight loss, using behavioral science to determine the specific weight loss program for each member. Before signing up for this program, you have several questions to answer because your answers help the company determine the cognitive behavioral therapy that will best suit each person.

The first thing you notice when landing on the website is that Noom does not call itself a weight loss program. Instead, they consider themselves a digital health company. This marketing tool comforts prospective customers when they see that they're taking a step toward improving their health, and the weight loss simply comes with it. It helps members build habits to last a lifetime.

While the website has more to explore than the other two online-only weight loss programs in this chapter, Noom follows many of the same marketing techniques used by many companies. However, as usual, it also veers off in a few places ,with just enough of a twist to interest new customers. For example,

## Ethos and Logos

Noom follows a science-based program, so much of their main website page is filled with information to explain the principles behind their business. This information is the ethos or credibility behind their program. Besides modeling pathos or emotional appeal, the testimonials also offer ethos and a bit of logos or logical reasoning. It's logical to assume that because a product or service has worked for others, it will also work for you. But the primary source of logos is the research articles that customers can find on the website. These articles explain the science behind weight gain and subsequent weight loss through the Noom program.

## Pathos

The emotional text on this main page is where you see pathos at work. This appeal to emotions about why they created this weight loss program takes up quite a bit of space. The background and history of the founders of Noom follow the text to offer further pathos, and back up the rest of their reasoning.

## Blog

Noom provides a blog for members and viewers of the website. So even online companies recognize that a blog is a great marketing tool.

## Press Releases

So many younger companies recognize how valuable the press can be to market their services or products. Noom is no exception. This company needs to use the press as its most valuable marketing tool. The science behind Noom sets it apart from the rest. Noom must take advantage of that. The media can help with that.

## Accessibility

Like all online-based programs, Noom uses the most vital of the 4 As of Marketing—accessibility. Offering a program like this, and giving access through a cell phone or computer, is a big marketing deal. Cell phones have become an integral part of everyone's world; nobody goes anywhere without their cell phones anymore. So to give customers the ability to access their personalized plan from anywhere using their phone is marketing at its best.

# Chapter 7

# WEIGHT LOSS COMPANIES WITH MEAL KITS

Traditionally, weight loss programs provided meals for their customers. While this leaves the hard work to the company rather than the client figuring out what to cook, it could also be inconvenient. Nevertheless, some weight loss programs today are still providing meals. For some, this program is convenient. The company has determined the number of calories per meal, and provides accordingly. Chapter 7 will cover a weight loss company that has been around for a while, and a couple using a newer meal kit program proven to be a big hit with customers. Let's see how these weight loss companies market this strategy.

## NUTRISYSTEM

Nutrisystem has been around since 1971, so its longevity is part of its excellent marketing strategy. People feel they can trust something that has stayed in business for so long. Other weight loss programs also use some of the same marketing techniques used by Nutrisystem, but there are some significant differences.

## Accessibility

Though differently, Nutrisystem has provided access to its customers in more than one way. The biggest is the meals Nutrisystem provides. Although for a price, Nutrisystem offers meals and snacks.

First, customers do not have to shop for groceries, because their meals get delivered. Second, because they receive meals, the customer does not have to plan a menu; a schedule is also part of the package. Third, the customer only needs to heat the fully prepared, prepackaged meals. This accessibility provides a level of convenience to the customer that many enjoy. Their busy lives do not include deciding what to eat, grocery shopping, or preparing a meal.

Another aspect of accessibility is the mobile app included with the program. Within this app, the customer can find their personalized plan, and the schedule for the delivered food. Combined, Nutrisystem offers accessibility that is difficult for customers to turn down.

## Engagement

The Nutrisystem website has a chat box at the bottom if a customer wants to ask questions or discuss their plan. This feature is a better marketing tool than one would think, since even though so many prefer to work on their meal plan from the comfort of their home, nobody wants to feel alone. It's like being lost at sea with nobody to help when questions arise.

## Testimonials

Of course, testimonials are always a standard of marketing, especially for weight loss programs.

## Ethos

The Nutrisystem program is credible. First, there is longevity, which builds trust and confidence in the company. Second, media sites that have showcased Nutrisystem's program at some point. Third, information is given throughout the site to prove this company knows what they're doing. Finally, research has been conducted, and studies have been performed, to show that its system works.

## Pathos

There are many happy people in the pictures on Nutrisystem's website. Between the photos and testimonials, Nutrisystem speaks to its customers' emotions.

# HELLOFRESH

HelloFresh began in 2011. It is not a weight loss program, although some food boxes cater to healthy eating. The meals that HelloFresh provides differ from the ones Nutrisystem provides its customers. HelloFresh includes specific ingredients with recipe cards to match. The idea is to promote less food waste, and encourage families to cook together, with the easy-to-follow recipes provided by the company.

The first marketing strategy that comes to mind is:

## Accessibility

Having groceries delivered has become common practice. HelloFresh offers groceries, but with a twist. Only the ingredients for specific recipes are delivered. There is no wasted food, no unnecessary groceries. The convenience of having your food delivered to your door is not lost on customers. The realization that you don't have to fight the lines in the grocery stores, or discover that your favorite brand of peanut butter is out of stock, is a relief.

Other marketing strategies HelloFresh uses are similar to those used by other weight loss companies. These are as follows:

## Blogs

No matter what you're selling, whether a service or a product, a blog offers that bit of pathos. As I've mentioned in a previous chapter, a company that cares enough to write a blog cares about its customers—what a great marketing tool!

## Press Releases

HelloFresh deals with food, and there are many rules about handling, shipping, and storing food. Therefore, it's a vital marketing tool to take advantage of the press, allowing them access to every aspect of the business. Doing so can prove the company goes above and beyond to ensure the safety of its customers.

## Ethos

HelloFresh lists the details of what goes in the various boxes, showing their knowledge and their credibility. In the question and answer portion, you get a glimpse of this credibility toward the bottom of the main website page. HelloFresh has done its homework, showing that all the information offered through the website increases the customer's feeling that they can believe and trust this company.

## Testimonials

Even though HelloFresh is not a weight loss program, testimonials are still a vital part of marketing. The company provides food to customers, so testimonials reassure prospective clients that the provided food is tasty. Customers need to know that the recipes will be easy to follow, and the meals simple enough to prepare. HelloFresh increases its credibility through these testimonials, because the reviews prove that the company is true to its word; hat what they say they provide is true.

## Pathos

Every time a company posts pictures on its website depicting happy customers, this is considered an appeal to emotions, and a powerful marketing tool. In addition, the testimonials include pictures of families cooking together, a definite appeal to the emotional side of any business.

Pathos can elicit another type of emotion besides happiness in a customer. HelloFresh has a sustainability program, and a commitment to diversity. Their mission and impact are of social responsibility. The emotions that come from learning about a company such as HelloFresh are the prominent reasons a prospective customer will become a member of this meal kit club.

# HOME CHEF

Home Chef is another meal kit club that does not fall under the weight loss program category. The company was started in 2013, making it another younger company providing meal kits to customers. I would like to point out that these last two companies, although not weight loss programs, have utilized one of the most critical marketing strategies: their founders saw a need and then met it. Food waste has become a significant issue in the United States, and someone saw an opportunity to offer busy families the exact amount of ingredients to prepare home-cooked, healthy meals. Of course, there are other ways the company utilizes some of the same marketing tactics the others use, but naturally with a twist. While companies follow the same pattern, they all know how important it is to stand out. Offering what the public wants but with a unique flair can put a company on top.

## Accessibility

As with HelloFresh, the convenience of meals delivered to your door is a marketing strategy that checks all the boxes. That makes the program accessible to customers because they skip the need to grocery shop. However, there is another way to look at it for accessibility and convenience. For a busy family, the ability to bypass stopping at the store to pick up groceries to make dinner saves time. This time-saving strategy means that Home Chef has allowed their families to spend more quality time together, which is another marketing strategy this book has covered. This is their appeal to emotion or pathos.

Another aspect of accessibility for Home Chef is how easy it is for customers to find the recipes on their website. A prospective customer who tries out a couple of them will most likely become a member to gain access to all the recipes.

Also similar to the weight loss programs is the ability to use a mobile app with this meal kit company. I think that at this point, it would be difficult to find a company that does not offer a mobile app with its services. Even grocery stores have mobile apps.

## Testimonials

Always and forever a marketing strategy that works, testimonials are essential to Home Chef's website. The testimonials are also recipe-specific, like a survey of "What was your favorite meal?" Because customers get to choose the recipes they want, many of Home Chef's recipes will stay in rotation.

## Engagement

There is a chat box at the bottom of the website's main screen, and a feedback button on the side. This feedback button could be one of the most essential marketing tools Home Chef could use. Especially since they're a pretty young company, it's necessary to continue to improve their product and service—what better way than asking customers to offer feedback? In addition, because this tab shows up even when you're not logged in, the company is willing to find out if they need to improve on anything that will also draw in new customers.

## Ethos

A banner midway down the website's main page offers numbers and statistics to prove Home Chef's credibility. This appeal to credibility for a company cannot be taken lightly. Every company needs to prove they're worth doing business with; otherwise, what is the point of being in business? There are multiple meal kit companies today, and each one must try and stand out. Ethos is a great way to accomplish this.

I have included Hello Fresh and Home Chef in the same chapter as Nutrisystem because of the meal kits. It is essential to note an important distinction between the companies, though. Because the meal kit companies offer selections that include healthy or calorie-conscious meals, they provide the same thing Nutrisystem offers. The difference is that meal kit companies are not promising you'll lose weight by choosing their meals.

Weight loss programs have become so varied today that I think it's important to note how their plans can be so similar to companies that don't sell weight loss but sell access to the same meal plans. Especially when it comes to marketing, the strategies used by each are identical and for the same reasons.

# Chapter 8

# WEIGHT LOSS COMPANIES WITH MULTIPLE GOALS

Some weight loss programs recognize the value of focusing on more than just losing weight. The programs covered in this chapter also provide supplements and products that cover the range of skincare, haircare, and overall healthcare. So it's the whole package with these companies.

One note, though, about overall health and wellness in weight loss companies. In several weight loss programs' information from earlier chapters, you'll notice that general health was a focus. This is becoming a regular feature of all weight loss programs. It is unusual to see a weight loss program that does not try to address the customer's overall health, usually through nutrition. The difference is that these three companies don't just call it weight loss; they overtly focus on the rest.

## BEACH BODY

Beach Body has existed since 1998, so it's not a young company. It has some longevity which, as I've noted before, is part of the marketing strategy. Companies with years and experience behind the name can use that as part of the appeal to their credibility or ethos. Most people are hesitant to do business with a company that doesn't have much of a track record. It's like purchasing a new software right after development. There's always the thought that letting the manufacturer figure out the kinks before spending the money is better.

Beach Body offers more than weight loss, although it is part of the program. It also provides in-home fitness and nutrition that includes meal plans and supplements. The company's credibility is in play because the website offers information about the science behind Beach Body's products. Based on experience and knowledge, Beach Body comes across as a credible source for the supplement the company creates and sells.

## Engagement

With a twist on this marketing strategy, Beach Body offers its members the opportunity to take advantage of its Fitness Live Streaming platform. In addition, the company also provides BODgroups, a direct connection to coaches to receive support while tracking progress. This marketing tool is a boost because although Beach Body is an in-home fitness program, these connections offer accountability to the member. Accountability is vital to member success when losing weight or engaging in a fitness program.

## Pathos

Beach Body's mission is based on social responsibility, to help people with more than fitness goals. The company's philanthropic pursuits appeal to emotions. So naturally, people want to be part of a program that strives for that kind of humanity.

Beach Body doesn't cater to just weight loss; it's a total fitness package with a broader target audience. A few more marketing tools the company uses are typical of any company trying to keep its members happy while gaining new ones. They are as follows:

- Blog
- Press Releases
- Shop: this is a new marketing strategy, but it's integral to this company's business methods. The shop is for customers to purchase supplies, equipment, and supplements, many created by Beach Body.

# GOLO

GOLO is also called the Golo Metabolic Plan, which indicates the intentions behind this weight loss program. GOLO was founded in 2009, so it is a pretty new company. However, no matter how unique, they utilize the same marketing techniques. But again, I can't stress enough how sometimes there can be a twist in a company's use of these tactics, and GOLO is no exception.

## Ethos

The name Golo Metabolic Plan is a clear indication of the company's credibility or ethos as a marketing strategy. Golo operates its business believing that most weight gain is due to insulin resistance. Therefore, the company has created a supplement to control insulin levels which regulates metabolism. The supplement is a proprietary blend of plant extracts and minerals, and the fact that it has been created explicitly for GOLO increases the level of credibility to customers. People trust science, and creating a product to assist in weight loss while possibly reducing the risk of diabetes and its health risks is significant.

## Accessibility

The GOLO website is easy to navigate, giving customers all the necessary information. However, some companies don't like tabs; they prefer their customers to stay on one central page. GOLO has utilized this philosophy, because while there are a few tabs, almost all the information about the company and its services is on the main website page.

There is also a mobile app for customers to download, making engaging with the company easier. And, of course, because the company has a supplement, there is a shop. Customers don't have to go to a store, or find the supplement on another website; it can be purchased right where they are. Keeping the customer on the same website to buy the product means they don't get distracted, which can lead to forgetting their goal of signing up. In addition, this marketing strategy increases the chance of gaining a new member of the GOLO club.

## Pathos

GOLO utilizes the appeal to emotion, as well, with its empowerment statement and program of working with the community to promote health and wellness. Then, the prospective customer finds pictures of the company's employees with families. This strategic use of the marketing tactic appealing to emotions gives the customer the impression that those employees will also feel like their family.

# ALIGN WEIGHT LOSS & BODY BALANCING

Align Weight Loss & Body Balancing was founded in 2014. It is a doctor-directed program designed to determine the deficiencies in your system that have blocked the ability to lose weight. Align is a weight loss program, but the company has an added process that helps you lose inches. It's called Body Contouring—red and infrared light penetrates the skin in photobiostimulation. The process releases fat cells that leave your body through the lymphatic system, while speeding up metabolism to control your hunger levels.

Probably the most effective marketing tool this program has is the ability to help the customer lose weight and inches without surgery. It can take a long time to reach your desired body size, and this program promises to get you there faster. Align still uses the same marketing techniques the rest of the weight loss programs use. For instance:

## Ethos

Align's credibility is assured once the potential customer reads the phrase doctor-directed on the website. The rest of the website's main page flows from there, with potential customers feeling more reassured as they read. Science is behind the philosophy, and for many, the fact that this company, while still relatively young, has been around for eight years soothes any unease about jumping into an untried program.

The weight loss tab adds to the credibility, which lays out the steps you'll take to lose weight. It lists each step, what to do, and, most importantly, why. For many, this offers stability and a sense of peace ,because they don't have to guess. In addition, this reduces the anxiety most people already have about any weight loss process.

## Social Media

Align is another weight loss program that recognizes the value of social media. It is no surprise that social media platforms offer such a rewarding marketing tool. So many people put their whole lives on social media sites, and a weight loss program will be one of the milestones covered. Seeing the before and after pictures on social media could not be a more effective marketing tool for Align.

## Testimonials

Align is not completely untried, though, because the website offers testimonials or, as they call them, Weight Loss Success Stories. These are the pieces of the program that reassure a customer. Because, as with anything else, if it worked for another person, it will work for you, right?

## Blog

Align is yet another weight loss program that utilizes the appeal to customers with a blog. That particular marketing strategy is an effective tool. Every click of the mouse, and every article read, is another step toward customers deciding to follow this program. There are recipes, and just about everyone trying to lose weight is looking for healthy recipes.

# Chapter 9

# RELIGIOUS-BASED COMPANIES

Some companies are not overtly religious; however, the founder usually is. They may not sell religion-based products, but they run their companies based on Christian fundamentals. Some treat their employees like family. Some donate their profits to help others, while some companies simply run their businesses using an innately religious philosophy. This chapter will highlight the highly successful companies that are not overt, but their faith is behind the marketing strategies they choose to employ.

One thing to remember about the marketing strategies of a company that has based its business practices on biblical principles is that marketing is a form of ministering. The act of ministering is to take care of someone's needs, and marketing tools are how you spread your message and meet those needs. Many Christian groups follow the teachings of Jesus and the Bible, which promotes Jesus as the ultimate example of how to minister to others. So, when someone uses the term 'ministering,' they are trying to represent Jesus, to follow His examples found within the Bible.

Therefore, when business owners say they're operating their business based on biblical principles, they're ministering through their business. The marketing techniques they practice will further that agenda. These principles usually indicate a significant community presence with vast philanthropic endeavors.

# IN-N-OUT BURGER

In-N-Out Burger began in 1948 and was exclusive to California. The founders, Harry and Esther Snyder, built the business based on some simple core values:

- cleanliness
- quality
- service

The couple possessed a commitment to quality with a reputation for excellence. They treated their associates like family, which has become a legacy inspired by a steadfast dedication to the restaurant chain's customers.

Esther Snyder was a woman of unwavering faith, and it was her faith behind the philanthropic work that has added to the company's legacy. As a result, In-N-Out Burger has created some inspiring foundations:

- Feed the Homeless Program
- INO Foundation, which began as the Child Abuse Fund
- Slave 2 Nothing Foundation

Indeed, the history of this company alone is a marketing technique that can only serve to inspire other companies. Thanks to the founders of In-N-Out Burger, this company has created a foundation of the "treat others as you would have others treat you," principle that has guided the company's path from the beginning. The business has grown with restaurants in seven states:

- California
- Nevada

- Arizona
- Utah
- Texas
- Oregon
- Colorado

Management of the company has stayed in the family, and recently one of the owners has had Bible verses printed on cups, containers, and wrappers. Of course, the placement is discreet, and you would have to look for them, but it's a testament to the faith that helped build the business. It is important to remember that the company does not blatantly promote religion. Instead, principles management possesses enable them to implement such effective marketing strategies.

# FOREVER 21

Forever 21 is a clothing store that supplies inexpensive products to the budget-conscious shopper. When done overtly and discreetly, it's not easy to recognize the religious marketing strategies that companies like this use. Forever 21 has John 3:16 printed on the bottom of all their shopping bags. At one point, the store tried to sell religious-themed tees, announcing things like

- Jesus ♥ You
- Holy

but received too much backlash from it.

According to an interview with the store owners, the family is religious, and they believe God told them to open the business, and they were promised success if they obeyed. It's difficult to know if the religious beliefs have created this clothing chain's success, but their marketing strategies are working. Affordable clothing is the main explanation behind the success, of course.

However, for a company that desires to implement religious beliefs, it stands to reason that they would incorporate a sense of inclusion and faith into their business practices. Further, it stands to reason that these practices would filter down their marketing strategies, relationships with employees, and customer commitment. When the customer feels loved, the company succeeds.

# ALASKA AIR

Alaska Air is a successful airline company that has been around since 1932. The company has undergone many changes over the years, but one thing has remained the same. Alaska Air has included an inspirational note-card with a passage from the Old Testament with their in-flight breakfast for decades.

The notecard is not intended to be a blatant religious move. Instead, it is the company's way of empowering the customer, of letting them know someone cares. The company recognizes that its customers are diverse, from all walks of life. Although they never intend to offend anyone, they firmly believe in the company's philosophy since the beginning: Customer first. To that end, Alaska Air employs some marketing techniques that we've talked about in the previous chapters.

## Accessibility

Alaska Air was the first airline to offer its customers self-bag-tagging. In addition, Alaska Air provides mobile apps, and accepts Google Wallet. Some people don't like to fly, and the experience has changed dramatically over the last few years. These features offer accessibility that helps smooth the process.

## Social media

Alaska Air is available on social media sites to foster customer communication.

Almost every marketing strategy Alaska Air utilizes within the company seems based on that basic outward appearance of faith. It shows in their practices, as well. Alaska Air respects the environment and its customer-first philosophy—the backbone of its company.

# HOBBY LOBBY

Hobby Lobby was founded in 1972, and has become a national arts-and-crafts chain store that operates "in a manner consistent with biblical principles" (Nielsen, 2013). Those biblical principles mean the company invests heavily in the community. The company's website also states they are committed to practicing company policies that build character, strengthen individuals, and nurture families (*Our Story*, 2019).

The commitments Hobby Lobby has made all fall under biblical principles. Most marketing experts say to choose a specific target audience, and we can see that all companies follow this advice. Hobby Lobby is no different; for example, its target audience comprises people who enjoy arts and crafts. However, when backing your marketing strategies with biblical principles, you can send a universal message, and it will reach a much larger audience (Christine, 2021). Hobby Lobby uses those biblical principles, so its message reaches more than just people who like arts and crafts. Their work in the community will bring in more customers who choose to give their business to a company with such human-centered values.

# MARTIN'S FAMOUS PASTRY SHOPPE, INC.

Martin's is a family-owned business that began 65 years ago. Their customer service policies are rooted in Christianity. The founders, Lloyd and Lois Martin, **may** have been religious, but whatever the reason, they chose to create their company using practices that could come straight out of the Bible. Consciously or unconsciously, Martin's ministers to customers, and this effort is evident in the company's business practices. As part of what could be considered biblical principles, Martin's has exceptional customer service.

According to its website, Martin's also has a strong community focus. The company gives back to its local communities with:

- service projects
- product donations
- contributions to nonprofits
- a portion of earnings donated to charities

There is something about this company that stands out from the others, though. Martin's is so devoted to keeping a solid ethical workplace that they have instituted an Ethics Hotline. They ask that if you know of illegal or unethical conduct performed by Martin's company, to report it. Since fairness and integrity are a part of this company's business practice, they are determined to keep it that way.

On top of the biblical marketing principles, this company has a few other tactics that are standard for businesses.

- Blog: Blogs can be a fun way to promote a business. Whether the company highlights its community service work or focuses on its employee family, a blog can create a personality.
- Social media: Since the company does not operate throughout the United States, social media is a smart way to create more visibility.
- Accessibility: This company operates exclusively on the east coast, so it has provided an online store to purchase products. However, the best part is the website recipes for using that product. In terms of accessibility, this is excellent. Living on the 'wrong' side of the US can be frustrating when there's an available product that is appealing. Businesses that offer an online shopping experience recognize customers' desires, and go out of their way to fulfill them.

As I will mention later, many of the marketing strategies used by companies are linked. One cannot be used without another, and so on. Martin's is an excellent example of this. The blog and the social media presence are all intertwined with accessibility. This company has taken its limited presence, and made the most of it. Their stores may only exist in part of the US, but their social media presence and blog have made them accessible to the rest of the United States. That is how marketing strategies are supposed to work.

# JETBLUE

JetBlue was founded in 1998, and for a long time, the founder and CEO of the company would sometimes greet boarding passengers while wearing a flight attendant apron. This is a unique customer service approach but important to JetBlue's owner. From his time as a Mormon missionary, he learned to treat everyone equally. While he did not put his religious beliefs into the company in an overt manner, he did take the ethics he learned from his church, and made them a part of the core values of JetBlue.

Based on the information I could get about the company, the marketing strategies I could readily see included the company's values, which were passed on to the customer. Of course, for many people, the reasons for using a specific airline are comfort, price, and accessibility. But the bottom line is how the people are treated. JetBlue was off to a great start in that area, since the owner did not like class distinction. Here is how I see he put that belief into effect with his company.

## Accessibility

JetBlue is a low-cost airline, but according to what I read, they don't skimp on passengers' comfort. Although the airline, like many, suffered setbacks through the years, the company only changed or adjusted parts of its operation to promote customer satisfaction. This, to me, is a big part of the owner treating everyone the same. As a result, profits did not outweigh customers' comfort and satisfaction with their flying experience.

## Values

According to JetBlue, the company's mission is to inspire humanity. Their five values of safety are:

- Safety
- Caring
- Integrity
- Passion
- Fun

All those values are important, but integrity stands out. The company's integrity passed through employees makes the company successful, and its passengers happy.

It's not just the passengers that are happy, though. According to research, JetBlue employees seem satisfied, and their retention is high. For example, the average time for an employee with Jetblue is 5.5 years. And whatever JetBlue does to promote happiness and retention among their employees seems to be working, since they make less than employees at other airlines.

# Chapter 10

# RELIGION-BASED COMPANIES USING CELEBRITY ENDORSEMENT

Successful marketers know that a product endorsed by a celebrity has the potential to make millions. When done correctly, the tactic known as Marketing with Celebrities can be a wildly successful venture. Celebrities lend weight to a product. You see it in commercials: Tom Selleck has been on TV for several decades and is viewed by many as a mature, level-headed, reliable individual. Of course, it helps that those are the types of roles he has played for several years. So, when the Reverse Home Mortgage Loan commercials air, hearing about it from someone like Selleck would make many people take notice. Maybe they'd even think twice about something they may not have thought was such a good idea, until they saw a celebrity like Tom Selleck endorsing the concept. Of course, it helps if you like the star, since few of us will rush out and buy something endorsed by a celebrity we don't like.

Marketers know it's important for the celebrity to have a certain level of credibility for viewers to show an interest in the product. You wouldn't necessarily buy a set of knives from someone like Ashton Kutcher, but you would if Gordon Ramsey was the celebrity endorser. Because, let's face it, nobody has seen Kutcher use a knife set on a cooking show.

The same is true for religious products endorsed by celebrities. There has to be credibility to encourage consumers to buy a religious product from someone who shows no outward level of Christianity. Nobody is looking to follow a hypocrite; we want to feel that the product is legit, and that only happens if the celebrity is also legit. The average consumer might hesitate to purchase a devotional book from someone like Alice Cooper. It would feel awkward, like it's all a big joke.

## CANDACE CAMERON BURE: CLOTHING LINE

It's no secret that Candace Cameron Bure is a devout Christian. She expresses her belief on air, and her on-screen persona is that of a wholesome, religious individual. She is a child star who has grown up in the movie/tv industry and has kept it simple, touting family and the love of God as what keeps her going and brings her success. Bure sells her clothing line on her website and QVC, but it's more than just clothing. She has stationary, gifts, skincare, books, and Bibles. Bure is selling more than just a product; she is selling a personality. She promotes inclusivity and woman empowerment, all through Jesus' love.

Bure is someone who has specifically put her name to a product, and has a say in the clothing styles she sells. When you see that she sells a t-shirt that says, "You are Precious in My Sight—God" with the Bible verse underneath, it does not leave a bad taste in your mouth. She is a celebrity who openly endorses Jesus daily, and is not afraid to do the same in her clothing line.

Bure uses ethos, an appeal to her character, as a marketing tool, whether she's doing it knowingly or not. Because the public is exposed daily to her Christian beliefs, we find that she is a credible source. Remember that Bure has not given the public reason to believe she is a hypocrite. The movies and shows she chooses are family-oriented and wholesome. Nothing scandalous in her personal life would give her fans reason not to trust her judgment. Therefore, consumers are willing to purchase her product because they can believe in Candace Cameron Bure.

She also uses pathos, an appeal to emotions, in her company. Through her years on *Full House*, we have watched her grow up. She has starred in countless Hallmark movies. She is open and honest about her faith, and when she struggles with depression or anxiety, she is open about turning to God to help her. She has invited us into her life as family, and the emotional attachment people feel drives them to purchase her product. Consumers stand by her because she feels real. Bure recognizes that it is her personality she is selling. Whatever takes place behind closed doors, her public persona brings customers back to her time and again.

## TIM TEBOW: LENDING HIS NAME TO SELL PRODUCTS

Tim Tebow is another celebrity who is openly religious. The football turned baseball star is vocal about what he believes. He used to put Bible verses on his eye black for football games in college. Unfortunately, the controversy surrounding that practice became so great that the NCAA had to ban players from writing anything on their eye black.

Tebow's commitment to his faith is so strong that he has become a celebrity endorser for several products, one of which is:

### Clean Juice

Founded in 2016, Clean Juice is dedicated to providing delicious, healthy, and organic products to communities (Juice, 2021). In 2021, Clean Juice accomplished two goals to market its business successfully. First, they have partnered with Tim Tebow, making him their first-ever national brand ambassador. He will essentially become the face of Clean Juice.

The plan is to put his face and name out there:
- National TV spot
- social media
- point-of-purchase materials
- product development

Clean Juice will capitalize on Tebow's unbending commitment to his beliefs, which will, in turn, uphold the company's core values. Tim Tebow is considered a source of inspiration literally for the world. His "passion for health and wellness" aligns perfectly with Clean Juice, whose core values are rooted in 3 John 1-2: "healthy body and a strong spirit" (Juice, 2021).

Through celebrity endorsement by naming Tebow as its national brand ambassador, Clean Juice can partner with the Tim Tebow Foundation. The philanthropic commitments of Tebow and Clean Juice are equal. Both are committed to aiding local communities by educating underprivileged kids about nutrition, while giving them access to organic eating and exercise. This is basically providing them the tools for overall wellness.

Like Candace Cameron Bure, Tim Tebow is a celebrity who does not shy away from expressing his religious beliefs. While there has undoubtedly been controversy around the sports star, it has not been caused by scandal. Just the opposite, in fact. Tebow stands out because he does not waver in his belief in a world that has largely denied a commitment to religion. He stands firm through criticism.

Tebow is like a rock, firm in his commitment to his faith. He has not faltered. Instead, he began the Tim Tebow Foundation to embody his authenticity, altruism, and genuine compassion for everyone.

As a marketing strategy, Clean Juice made an excellent choice when it partnered with Tebow to offer dedicated community service. It makes sense for a company to market its services and product through celebrity endorsement, especially when that celebrity shares its values and beliefs.

Because of Clean Juice's commitment to the community, and the desire to help with nutrition, its marketing strategies look like a focus on reaching out to as many people as possible. Therefore, Clean Juice also utilizes other marketing techniques such as:

- blog
- social media
- TV ads with Tim Tebow as their national brand ambassador

The company can count on success through the use of celebrity endorsement by associating with someone like Tim Tebow: respected man, admired and liked by so many.

# CARRIE UNDERWOOD: ENDORSING A PRODUCT AS WHOLESOME AS SHE IS

Carrie Underwood is unapologetically religious, with a wholesomeness about her that promotes health and wellness. It's no wonder, then, that she has been chosen to endorse a product that promotes that same health and wellness. This is the case of a religious celebrity endorsing a product that is not overtly religious. However, the product promotes some of the same qualities that the celebrity generally promotes.

## BodyArmor

BodyArmor has used endorsers in the past: all sports stars such as James Harde, Megan Rapinoe, and Naomi Osaka. But now, Carrie Underwood will be the first celebrity endorser of this product that has been focused on the sports world and athletes for years. In addition, BodyArmor promotes healthy hydration, which aligns with Underwood's personal mission of health and wellness.

The company wants to broaden its target audience. They're looking to expand out of the sports world, and Carrie Underwood's image is just what the company needs. Underwood has a wholesome image that will readily promote the company's product. However, BodyArmor recognizes that Underwood's appeal will reach more people who would not normally consider purchasing a sports drink. She is a mom and a very active mom.

Celebrities prefer to endorse a product they can believe in, that aligns with their personal beliefs or goals. Therefore, the choice of Carrie Underwood to endorse BodyArmor's sports drink can only be viewed as a wise decision to promote a company that promotes the same values she possesses. Aside from hiring a celebrity endorser, BodyArmor uses other marketing tools to promote its company. Let's take a look at what they are.

## Transparency

Carrie Underwood is transparent about her belief system, and BodyArmor is transparent about its product. Because they sell bottled water, the company must meet FDA standards of quality. To promote transparency and instill trust in its customers, BodyArmor posts its quality reports.

## Social Media

BodyArmor is a company that regularly utilizes endorsers for its product, so it would also make sense to market itself through social media.

## Press Releases

I can't say enough about the media as a marketing tool. Social media and press releases are two marketing tools that go hand-in-hand with celebrity endorsers. Celebrities are in the public's eye, and Carrie Underwood is no exception. Underwood cannot escape the media in her eighth year as the theme song-singer for Sunday Night Football. As with the case of all celebrity endorsers, every time the media promotes Underwood, they're promoting BodyArmor.

# Chapter 11

# IT'S ALL ABOUT SELLING RELIGION

Some companies sell only religious products, and you'll find many with an online presence only. However, you've seen by now that every company, no matter what they sell, has a significant online presence, and selling religion is no different. Furthermore, you've already seen how the sale of faith has become a significant player in commerce, with celebrity-endorsed products. So let's look at how companies sell religious-based products without a celebrity, especially with a narrow target audience, since all products have a religious theme.

It might be a good idea to mention here that experts recommend narrowing your target audience a little. It's natural to want to sell to everyone when you go into business, but that's not very realistic. Everybody doesn't like everything. So selling religion-based products has a narrow target audience, but is not too narrow. For instance, you might not be religious, but maybe Aunt Mabel is. Christmas is right around the corner, so naturally, the best place to shop for Aunt Mabel is at a Christian bookstore, or checking out Christian products online.

We must also remember that this particular category will have a few different marketing strategies. The websites are just big stores online, and what better way to bring in customers than to offer sales or discounts. But let's see what marketing strategies these online religion-based product companies use.

# CHRISTIANBOOK.COM

Christianbook.com is the online presence of Christian Book Distributors, a brick-and-mortar store. The original store was started in 1978 by two brothers, and the website, Christianbook.com, was launched in 1996.

When you enter the website, you are greeted with a pop-up asking if you'd like to sign up with your email and be notified of deals, free shipping events, and special sales. This is a marketing technique that, while it might be annoying, is effective in keeping the company's name in front of potential and existing customers.

As expected, there are several marketing strategies this company shares with other companies, such as:
- Social media
- Blog

Others are the same, but Christianbook.com has a slightly different approach. For example:

## Accessibility

It's a given that Christianbook.com will be accessible to all customers, since they are an online presence. However, they have increased their accessibility while widening their target audience.

In 1997, Christianbook.com expanded its product line to begin marketing directly to homeschoolers. This increased their target audience, while making their product available to more people. Another way the company made itself more accessible to customers was to add "Homeschool Compass" to its site map. Not only did they begin selling homeschool curricula, but they created a page specifically for homeschoolers. This page has a wealth of information for homeschool families:

- New to homeschooling: Navigating the world of homeschooling can be tricky and downright overwhelming. Christianbook.com aims to make it easier by answering their questions and offering advice.
- Free printables: Many homeschool families are unsure where to get practice sheets or worksheets. Christianbook.com offers many of them free of charge. This is a nice something to get a new homeschool family started.
- Finding your style: Many homeschool families have no idea what they're doing, let alone how they're doing it. The tips and ideas Christianbook.com has to offer will help a family make some choices.
- Organization: The worst is figuring out what you have to save, how to notate grades, and keeping transcripts together. There is so much paperwork! But it looks like Christianbook.com has the answers. And, of course, they can guide the family toward purchasing exactly what they need.

This page has many more categories, but is a huge marketing tool. Homeschool families will continue purchasing curriculum materials from Christianbook.com because the company offers excellent information.

## Engagement

I believe one link falls into the marketing strategy of customer engagement. It is labeled "Prayer Wall," and you are allowed the opportunity to write your prayer when you enter. The prayers people have written are all there, giving the customer the chance to pray for them all, or some, or whatever it is they feel called to do. But it is a form of engagement, the company showing they care, and that they're a family that takes care of each other.

Christianbook.com does have a few offers that are marketing tools. They are:

- Gift cards: What a way to gain new customers! This marketing tool is a way to broaden your target audience because, suddenly, people who might not usually purchase from the website are checking it out. And once they've made their first purchase, they may be back, and you've got a repeat customer.

- Membership: For a small fee, you can become a member and receive extra discounts when available.

- Self-publishing: Christianbook.com has a link to a book proposal service. This might sound odd, but the company's beginning was just selling books. So they sell a lot of religious texts. Naturally, they're going to want to add books to their inventory, and what better way to do that than to promote the writers of those books. It's a very clever marketing tool.

These extra marketing tools are going to be more common in retail companies.

## THE CATHOLIC COMPANY

The Catholic Company was founded in 2001, the week after September 11, 2001. This company's motivation behind the start was in answer to Pope St. John Paul II's call for Catholics to join the New Evangelization. The Catholic Company believes that the solution to the world's problems is a closer relationship with God and the Catholic church. This background in the company's formation and belief system sets the tone for its target audience. This target audience is a little narrower than the other religion-based companies. Not only is the company selling religion, but they're selling products proprietary to a specific religion.

This particular online retailer shows its affiliation to a specific religion in more than one way. First, there is the name. When customers look for religious-based products and see the name of this online business, they know they will get some items specific to the Catholic religion. The title leads to expectations, and that is a marketing strategy. If someone is looking for a rosary, then a Catholic store is assuredly going to supply it.

The website looks a little different, and is part of this company's marketing technique. A specific religion operates the business, so they will make the website comfortable for members of the Catholic church, offer incentives, and engage with customers through particular rituals.

For instance, tabs across the top will take you to various aspects of this company. One, in particular, is the strategy:

## Engagement

Although the engagement of this tab is not live-streaming or interactive in any way, it engages with the customer through a shared belief, and the rituals that come with that belief. The tab is "Morning Offering," and within it, you'll find items like

- Today's meditation
- Daily verse
- Daily mass readings
- Saint of the day
- Liturgy of the hours
- Monthly devotion

More tabs along the top take you to places like "Get Fed: Bite-sized faith," and this one is filled with fun facts about the Catholic church. For example, a box says, 'Why does the church use candles?' Many of these would be entertaining for customers who are not Catholic.

The website shares its core values in the "Our Story" section, connecting with customers whether they are Catholic or not. The "Great

Eight," as they are called, can be considered essential values, regardless of your religion.

This website offers a couple of examples of marketing strategies that are the more common ones you'll find

- Blog
- Reviews (outside the world of retail, this would be labeled testimonials)

It seems like the majority of marketing tools the Catholic Company uses are ones that create a connection to their customers through the marketing tool Engagement. This company also has a rewards program, another form of engagement or connection.

# CONCORDIA SUPPLY

Concordia Supply was founded in 1949, and the company moved to its online presence in 2001. They aim to provide products and supplies to churches and ministries, to help them do the Lord's work. Whichever religion is the basis for this company's goals, it is not blatantly evident. Most of the product is more appropriate for churches or ministries needing bulk items, such as offering envelopes.

I saw very few marketing strategies on this website; they may not need too many since their target audience is small. Catering to churches and ministries means that once a church or ministry has become Concordia's customer, they are probably long-term. However, they do have a few.

## Rewards Program

This is only the second company that I have noticed with a rewards program. However, many retail companies are implementing this program into their business, which seems to work. If customers know they will earn points that give them a discount or lower prices daily, they will usually become loyal customers.

Some of the marketing tools that I noted, but are common among all the companies discussed in this book, are these:

- Reviews (testimonials): Because this company states that its goal is to help churches and ministries by supplying products and resources, it's probably not the product that gets reviewed. It is the service and customer service which is a testimonial toward the company itself.
- Social media
- Special offers
- Missions and ministries: Concordia works with quite a few missions; this is another way for the company to connect with its customers. If a church sees the company's connection with another church or a mission, they develop a rapport and trust with the business.

Some of the services Concordia offers their customers are custom printing and design. They sell, design, and print resources like bulletins, banners, and other products.

I did see a product that looked exciting: VBS 2022. Concordia lists all the VBS themes for 2022 and what is included, giving churches the chance to purchase the kit they're interested in. It looked like a lot of fun, and since it includes children, it's sure to bring in some business.

## CROSSWALK

Some companies sell religion, but in a different format. Rather than selling religious-themed products, some companies sell religion as a service. I'm not talking about churches, but about the overall Christian life. For example, Crosswalk is an online magazine founded in 1993 for Christian living. The website offers everything a Christian needs to further their faith, and how to incorporate religion into their daily lives. With that in mind, let's go over the marketing tools this company uses to sell information and advice.

## Content Curation

Pop-up style ads slide over from the left side of the screen periodically, looking to capture your attention. The website is looking to gather your email address in exchange for a free guide or coloring pages, whatever the offer is at that moment. Pay attention to the fine print at the bottom of the pop-up. When you hit submit, you're giving the company permission to send special offers and daily updates to your inbox.

## Mobile App

As usual, this goes along with Accessibility. Crosswalk is a magazine, but it's an online magazine. So, naturally, the company wants you to access it at home or on the go. So, you're going to need it on your cell phone. Therefore, you can get the mobile app, which will allow you to read up on any subject you may need assistance with, no matter where you are.

## Automation

At the bottom of the page is a list of subjects offered by other companies on Crosswalk's parent company. Crosswalk is a subsidiary of a more extensive network, and similar topics are available on these other websites. The links are offered for the customer who might be looking for additional information.

## Accessibility

Of course, the online presence of this website makes it accessible. Crosswalk calls itself a magazine, and it's much more convenient to access it through the internet versus buying a paper copy of a magazine. One of the best features of an online magazine like this is that you don't have to keep the whole thing to get what you want. How many of you have back copies of magazines you're not willing to part with, because of that one article or recipe you just have to have? The magazines sit around collecting years of dust, and you don't even remember which articles you wanted, and you've never made the recipe. These online magazines create less clutter, and you can quickly access whatever it is you want to keep.

## Social Media and Newsletters

Crosswalk markets its online magazine through Facebook and Twitter, but the biggest thing I see that I would call social media is its Newsletters, with a twist. It is up to you, the customer, to determine what kind of newsletter you want to receive in your inbox. There are various topics and themes to choose from, and you can even select more than one. So if the only reason you're interested in this website is the advice on religion in your marriage, then you're going to choose that category. It's a great idea to customize the newsletter process. It gives the customer a real feeling of personalization, and there's not as much stuff to sort through to get what interests you the most.

## Blogs, Videos, Podcasts

This online magazine offers something everyone can enjoy. If you don't want to read, there are podcasts to listen to. Or you can just sit back and watch a video. Or you can read the articles that appeal to you. Either way, everyone's needs are met.

## News

Sometimes, when you feel you cannot absorb any more news, you can choose the kind of news you receive in this online magazine, Crosswalk. You can choose to read the top headlines or just read community news, which I would assume does not mean your physical community, but your spiritual community: information about others who believe the way you do.

## Ethos

The writers for Crosswalk are experts in their fields. Therefore, they write articles for their chosen field of expertise.

There is so much to choose from on Crosswalk's website. The selections include stuff like

- Podcasts
- Marriage
- The single life
- Parenting
- Homeschool
- Finance
- Career
- Youth Ministry
- Giving
- Worship
- Leadership
- Bible study
- Prayer
- Women
- Men
- Seniors

There are lists of recommended books, movies, and music. One whole section is devoted entirely to devotional podcasts, and that list is long.

Crosswalk is determined to sell a way of life, and its website has covered every topic one can think of. Unfortunately, you cannot read some of the articles unless you subscribe to the website. Although many people will be fine just reading the free articles, many people want all of the information. When you feel that your life is made better by the information you're getting from the website, you think the subscription cost is worthwhile.

# Chapter 12

# SELLING RELIGION IN NICHE MARKETS

et's face it; times are changing. With the changing times comes a change in how we do things, including marketing a business. The following companies are a little unique in some of their approaches, because they sell products for a niche market. But what is a niche market, you ask? Well, it's a small portion or segment of the market with a unique need or preference.

There are pros and cons to marketing your product for a niche market, and the top pro is brand loyalty. For example, if you sell only pastel ceramic 6-inch angel statues with one arm, the four people looking for that specific product will buy only from you,  because where else are they going to find what they need? They will be loyal to your company because you have met their unique needs and preferences.

Marketing is considered more accessible by some when selling to niche markets, because the product is so specific that you don't have to 'sell' anything; it practically sells itself. But some consider it a little more complicated, since marketing to bring in new customers might be challenging. In addition, when you know your target audience, it can be tough to learn how to market to sell to another group. Besides, how often do those four people want or need a one-armed angel statue?

So, there's a lot to consider when selling to a niche market, but the main question is whether the same marketing tools apply. For example, selling a service like weight loss programs or religious products is a niche market, but not as small as the ones in this chapter. There are a lot of religions to consider, but many people are religious in some way so the religion-based market is broader. And since most of the population feel they need to lose weight or get healthy, niche markets such as weight loss companies actually have a wider audience with a more generalized need. But let's look at the companies in this chapter and see how they adapt their marketing tools to meet their needs.

## ALABASTER:

Alabaster began in 2017, and the company has piqued my interest. I had to ask myself how Bible sales for this fledgling company could be up 21%. Aren't Bibles sold everywhere, and don't most people already have a Bible? That may be what many people think when they learn of this company, but if you dig a little deeper, there is a lot to unpack about its unique approach to Bibles. There are a couple of descriptions that I thought embodied the mission and objective of this company. So, to quote a little blurb from the founders, Brian Chung and Bryan Ye Chung:

> "Living in a more visually-centric generation, we judge a company by how their website looks," Chung says. "We were interested in exploring that in a faith-based context" (Koenig, 2022).

> "We integrate visual imagery and thoughtful design into different books of the Bible. We believe in the divine inspiration, trustworthiness, and authority of the Bible—and we bring this

into everything we make and do. We knew that the story of God was beautiful, and we wanted to create a beautiful reading experience—we ultimately hope it helps deepen your experience with God" (*Our Story,* n.d.).

The product is visually stunning, making me even more curious to check out their marketing techniques. Here is what I think about what I've discovered.

It's challenging to name some of the creative marketing strategies Alabaster employs to bring awareness to its product. Not surprising, since the company has its finger on the pulse of its niche target audience. Naturally, the company would like everyone to purchase their Bibles, but it's 2022—new territory for us all.

Alabaster must think outside the box and think on their feet, but more importantly, they must change the rules a little. It looks like they're doing just that. Some marketing strategies will be familiar, but some will sound unusual. But they all make sense when you realize that Alabaster's target audience is the newer generations.

These are millennials operating a business whose niche target audience is other millennials, their Gen-Y peers.

## Accessibility

Some marketing strategies are the same as other companies, because some things do not change. Online ordering is one of the top tools for accessibility when it comes to marketing. Another accessibility tool is the packaging of the product itself. To millennials, the Bible may not seem accessible; it's viewed as old-fashioned, patriarchal, or even narcissistic. But package it up the way Alabaster has, and you've got something that suddenly feels accessible, even desirable to the younger generations. They can purchase the books of the Bible they're interested in, and leave the rest for later. In this form, the Bible works into this younger group's lives and homes; it's possibly even hip.

## Press Releases

Nothing says look at me more than some good press, of course, and Alabaster recognizes and knows that only too well. So they will advertise the words right off those Bibles through press releases. This is especially so since the company is trying to market their Bibles as an expression of faith, but it's the expression Millenials want to make. Design is the key to this product, and the minimalist aesthetic could be taken right from hipster magazines and brands with the hipster vibe. Design needs to be seen, and the press is the best place to be seen.

## Influencers

Influencers can be a strategic marketing tool along with social media. Alabaster is targeting a niche audience of Millenials, and influencers are the ticket to everything with that generation. Makeup, recipes, food, DIY projects, everything you can think of has an influencer selling it to Millenials. The younger generation doesn't need a TV commercial to sell a product; they just need TikTok or Instagram, and an influencer.

## Social Media

Since the founders of Alabaster are Millenials, it makes sense that they will market their product on a few more social media sites than we've seen in some of the other companies in this book. These include
- TikTok
- Spotify

According to the founders of Alabaster, they use social media and influencers as a marketing tool and customer service. Of course, that is a different slant on social media usage, but when you think about it, it's logical. Millennials communicate via social media more than any other generation; if Alabaster is any indication, it's the future of customer service.

## Partnerships

This category might fall under accessibility, since partnering with some companies listed on its website makes the product more available. These partnerships are opportunities for customers to purchase the product:

- Meditation programs
- Bible project publication
- Year of the Bible national campaign
- Culture Care movement with video series
- Hillsong Team Box—monthly subscription

The monthly subscription boxes are becoming more popular, and I think they're a pretty savvy marketing tool. Of course, the customer never knows what they'll get, but it's a great way to generate brand loyalty.

## Impact: Philanthropy

Alabaster follows up its belief system and core values to work with programs and foundations like Feeding America and PS Arts. Since one of their goals is community outreach, these organizations help them reach their goals.

## Ethos

Besides the product, what stands out about Alabaster is that they employ ethos as a marketing tool. The company believes in authenticity, mainly because it is a faith-based product it sells. So the profoundly religious founders tapped into their credibility, and combined the two things they knew, to sell two products as old as time: the Bible and beauty.

# KINGSTONE MEDIA GROUP

Kingstone Media Group began in 2004, and is part of Kingstone Studios and Kingstone Comics. Another niche group, this company targets a younger audience. This is a tiny niche target audience, since the product is so specific in content and application. Really, you can't get any more niche than comic books about the Bible. Its target audience could also include a few older generations, except that its graphic novels and comics contain such a specific subject matter.

Kingston Media or Kingstone Comics creates fast-paced action adventure Bible comics and graphic novels, except that it's not just the Bible, but graphic novels and comics about faith. The company also has a *101 Questions About the Bible and Christianity* series. There is clothing in the online store, as well, with graphic novel-style images. At first glance, these images could be superheroes, but they are actually biblical characters like:

- Samson
- Moses
- David and Goliath

The marketing strategies employed by the Kingstone Media Group look pretty basic. This is due to the very narrow target audience they are trying to reach. However, Kingstone does perform philanthropic work due to their religious beliefs of giving back and helping others.

The founder, Art Ayris, is a pastor, and helped found The Community Medical Care Center, a no-cost clinic for the medically indigent. Giving back to the community and helping others is a marketing boost for companies like Kingstone. In addition, these practices enhance their belief system, boosting customers' interest in the company.

## Social Media

Kingstone Media is on many social media platforms, the same ones most companies are on. It's my opinion that the reason many companies embrace social media platforms as a marketing tool is because of the audience that relies on social media. You must search the customers out to reach markets that would not usually purchase your product. Getting your product or service on social media is the first and best way to do just that.

## Accessibility

Again, Kingstone Media uses the most fundamental aspect of accessibility in its marketing strategies. However, these aspects of accessibility are probably the most vital components.

- Online ordering: One of the first things a customer does is check a website to see if online ordering is available. If the product is too difficult to acquire, you will lose customers. Word spreads quickly about stuff like that.
- Newsletter: When purchasing books or anything in a series, having access to the news about upcoming titles is critical. Customers will devour a newsletter looking for news of release dates.
- Brick-and-mortar sales: sometimes, you get customers who don't want to wait for their product to be shipped. To know they can run down to the Christian bookstore or Barnes and Noble to buy the product will be a relief.

## Ethos

The Kingstone Media Group uses ethos as a marketing tool, a very effective marketing tool. For example, the website for Kingstone Comics states that the creators of their comic books and graphic novels have worked with Marvel or DC. That kind of background lends to the credibility of Kingstone products.

So far, these companies that market to such a narrow niche don't utilize as many marketing strategies as we've seen in other companies. But I think that's pretty common. Their marketing tools are sufficient to reach their small target audience, and remember, brand loyalty is its own strategy. You've done your job if you can meet their specific needs.

## 316TEES

316Tees is a company founded in 2013 by a US Army veteran. A deeply religious man, he and his family have made their religious beliefs the backbone of this company that produces only T-shirts. Besides religious messages, the company has incorporated patriotic messages into its T-shirt design. According to the website, 316Tees' mission is to help Christians "be the light of the world" (Robinson, 2021).

The founders of 316Tees could have decided to sell a complete clothing line with the tees, but they chose to focus strictly on T-shirt sales. This decision is what put them into the niche company. As a niche product, 316Tees also employs the marketing strategies significantly associated with this type of business.

## Ministering

316Tees states that their T-shirt line is inspired by truth. Through that truth, others will see the light in them. That truth will minister to others and lead them to follow Jesus, as well. Therefore, 316Tees ministers to the world through the messages on their tees and the love and truth to be seen in the company's message, or their mission.

316Tees also ministers to the world through their partnerships with other companies, such as

- One Kingdom Ministry: This ministry works on a different scale than the rest. Rather than sending missionaries to other parts of the globe, each sector of One Kingdom works within their nations and communities, bringing relief to their homefront.
- Coreluv: A team of believers whose mission is to rescue orphans while bringing Jesus's love to them.

## Social Media

Social media is not the most robust marketing strategy that 316Tees uses. However, as a marketing expert, the company's founder recognizes the value of even the most basic use of social media as a marketing tool.

## Blog

316Tees' blog posts are all centered around religion. This is an excellent way to continue ministering as part of their marketing strategies. Not only does the blog connect customers with the company, but it reiterates and confirms the faith behind the company. This confirmation of faith boosts the process of ministering to the customer.

## Ethos

Credibility when it comes to faith is not easy to do. It can be done, as we've seen in the chapter about celebrity endorsements. However, these niche market businesses are not usually run by a celebrity. Therefore, the customer truly has no idea what the business owner believes, outside of what they post on their website.

However, with regard to 316Tees, there is credibility in the owner of the business. He is a US army veteran, which gives credibility to the patriotic-themed T-shirts. Now, because of this, human nature being what it is, we can easily extend that trust to the issue of faith. So credibility has been established, and 316Tees has successfully added another marketing tool to their toolbox.

## Accessibility

As an online company, 316Tees has immediately established accessibility with their product. Not only is their product offered strictly online, but the company is operated by a veteran. So, of course, that means the company offers discounts to veterans—another point of accessibility for their product.

316Tees, then, is a niche market business because they sell only T-shirts. They have not added a full clothing line or accessories. What makes this company stand out in their market is that the T-shirts they sell are specific to religion. Therefore, if a customer is looking for a religious or patriotic T-shirt, this is the company they will investigate first, because they know they can probably find what they're looking for.

# CONCLUSION

Advertising can be a tricky thing. First, find a product, and decide on your target audience—not too big!—then figure out how you will sell that product to the people you're sure will buy it. So much risk, yet so much reward.

The name of your store, product, or service is an excellent place to start. Nothing draws the attention of customers like a catchy name or title. For example, I have wandered into many stores just because the name got my curiosity, and sometimes I've even bought.

There are many options for businesses to market their services or products, but I find the most interesting is how the marketing strategies can change due to the nature of the business. For example, we've seen that religion-based products have a few differences in their marketing tools. But we've also noticed that niche-based companies narrow their marketing tools even more.

What I find interesting is that there are some marketing strategies you would think would be exclusive to financial institutions, such as Self-Service and Digitization. Still, I think it's a tool that various companies can use. Then there are the marketing strategies used by niche-based businesses. Based on what we found, it looks like they don't use nearly the same level of marketing. Maybe that's because they already have brand loyalty within their customer base, since their product is so select.

What it comes down to is brand loyalty, and it is not exclusive to niche-based companies. If you can apply effective marketing strategies, you can build the brand loyalty you're looking for. We all know those people who only shop at one store because it carries the brands they prefer. I have friends who will travel out of their way to go to the grocery store they like, because it has specific brands of groceries they want. It is too anxiety-inducing for them to try another brand, so they shop where they're most comfortable.

That is another aspect of marketing: comfort. Whether your business is online or brick-and-mortar, if your customers are comfortable, they'll keep coming back. Comfort can include anything from your store's ambiance to your employees' friendliness and helpfulness. I have a friend who won't shop in crowded stores. She's terrified she's going to break something, so even if that store carries her favorite brand of soap, which it does, she still won't go in. She's not comfortable.

I noticed something while laying out the marketing strategies for each company in this book. Every tactic, technique, and tool connects like a puzzle. It's difficult to see where one strategy ends, and another begins. When these companies successfully create their marketing strategies, one thing leads to another. Therefore, you cannot have one tool, such as Digital Storytelling, without another, like Engagement.

Ethos ⇒ Logos ⇒ Pathos ⇒ Digital Storytelling ⇒ Accessibility ⇒Social Media ⇒ Testimonials ⇒ Blogs ⇒ Customer Outreach ⇒ Engagement ⇒ Press Releases ⇒ Surveys ⇒ Affordability ⇒ Celebrity Endorsements ⇒ Influencers ⇒ Self-Service and Digitization ⇒ Automation and Big Data ⇒ Events ⇒ Public Relations ⇒ Case Studies

Before setting up your marketing techniques, there are a few things to remember:

- Identify your individuality. What sets your product or service apart from your competitors?
- Know your target audience. Determine what it is your customers want and need.

- Keep your options open. Remember, you may need to adapt your marketing strategy if you find that your target audience has changed, or your ideas need a creative boost.
- Know your enemy. No, this is not war, but you'll need to do some research on your competitors. For example, how do they advertise, what marketing strategies do they employ, and what are their weaknesses?
- Don't exceed your budget. Keep track of your marketing expenses, then track how the marketing affects sales. It doesn't do to operate at a loss before you begin.

There's a lot to running a successful business, but you're set if you can get your marketing strategies in place. Then it's just a matter of updating them when the economy or technologies change. But a firm foundation of good marketing can help you become successful in your business.

# References

Alaska Airlines. (2019). *History|Alaska Airlines*. Alaska Airlines. https://www. alaskaair.com/content/about-us/history/history-by-decade

Bhasin, H. (2021, June 30). *4 A's of Marketing Explained With Their Types*. Marketing91. https://www.marketing91.com/4-as-of-marketing/

*Bringing Art to the People in Richmond*. (n.d.). www.jpmorganchase.com. https://www.jpmorganchase.com/news-stories/bringing-art-to-the-people-in-richmond

Chaffey, D. (2021, May 12). *Investment banking marketing strategies to win more customers. Smart Insights*. https://www.smartinsights.com/digital-marketing-strategy/investment-banking-marketing-strategies-to-win-more-customers/

Chen, J. (2020, May 12). *Learn What an Investment Company Is*. Investopedia. https://www.investopedia.com/terms/i/investmentcompany. asp#:~:text=The%20main%20business%20of%20an%20 investment%20company%20is

Christine. (2021, June 17). *The Biblical Principles of Marketing: Why You Should Promote Your Church*. Viral Solutions. https://viralsolutions. net/biblical-principles-of-marketing/

*Commitment to Inclusion, Diversity and Equity*. (n.d.). Edward Jones. https:// www.edwardjones.com/us-en/why-edward-jones/about-us/corporate-citizenship/inclusion-equity-diversity-commitments

Dodd, D. (2015, February 9). *For Effective Marketing, you Need both the 4A's and the 4P's|Customerthink*. Customerthink.com https:// customerthink.com/for-effective-marketing-you-need-both-the-4as-and-the-4ps/

Juice, C. (2021, July 20). *Tim Tebow Signs with Clean Juice As National Brand Ambassador*. www.prnewswire.com. https://www.prnewswire.com/ news-releases/tim-tebow-signs-with-clean-juice-as-national-brand-ambassador-301337086.html

Koenig, R. (2022, April 13). *Selling Bibles to Young People: How One Company Created a Niche Market for Fancy Bibles*. Blog.hubspot.com. https:// blog.hubspot.com/the-hustle/selling-bibles-to-young-people-how-one-company-created-a-niche-market-for-fancy-bibles

Nedrow, R. (2021, November 5). *20 Marketing Tactics That Work and How To Use Them (With Examples)*. Indeed Career Guide. https://www.indeed.com/career-advice/career-development/marketing-tactics

Niesen, M. (2013, June 13). *18 Extremely Religious Big American Companies*. Business Insider. https://www.businessinsider.com/18-extremey-religious-big-american-companies-2013-6

*Our Story*. (n.d.). Alabaster Co. https://www.alabasterco.com/pages/our-story

*Our Story*. (2019). Hobby Lobby. https://www.hobbylobby.com/about-us/our-story

Reed, E. (2020, February 24). *History of IBM: Timeline and Facts*. TheStreet. https://www.thestreet.com/personal-finance/history-of-ibm

Robinhood. (2022). About Us. Robinhood. https://robinhood.com/us/en/about-us/

Robinson, B. (2021, December 22). *"Top 10 Christian Clothing Brands"|Updated*. 316Tees. https://www.316tees.com/blogs/316/top-10-online-christian-clothing-stores#:~:text=Kerusso%2C%20Elly%20%26%20Grace%2C%20316Tees%2C%20God%20The%20Father

*The 5 Most Effective Marketing Strategies for Financial Services*. (2018, September 18). EVERFI. https://everfi.com/blog/financial-education/5-effective-financial-services-marketing-strategies/

*Tim Tebow - Clean Juice*. (2021, November 3). https://www.cleanjuicec.com/tim-tebow/

Triest, A. (2022, April 4). *What is Cryptocurrency and Should Your Business Use It?* StartupNation. https://startupnation.com/trending/what-is-cryptocurrency-should-business-use-it-triest/

*What is cryptocurrency and how does it work?* (2022, February 26). https://gulfofficial.com/blog/what-is-cryptocurrency/#:~:text=%E2%80%9CA%20cryptocurrency%20is%20an%20electronic%20cash%20system%20that

*Working At JetBlue Airways: Employee Reviews and Culture*. (2020, may 18). Zippia.com. https://www.zippia.com/jetblue-airways-careers-6348/